Our War Was Different

Our War Was Different

Marine Combined Action Platoons in Vietnam

Al Hemingway

Naval Institute Press ★ Annapolis, Maryland

Printed in the United States of America on acid-free paper

LIBRARY OF CONGRESS CATALOGING-IN-PUBLICATION DATA
Hemingway, Albert, 1950–
    Our war was different : Marine combined action platoons in Vietnam/
Al Hemingway.
        p.   cm.
    Includes bibliographical references and index.
    ISBN 1-55750-355-9
    1. Vietnamese Conflict, 1961–1975—Personal narratives, American.
2. United States. Marine Corps—History—Vietnamese Conflict,
1961–1975. I. Title.
DS559.5.H45 1994
959.704'38—dc20   93-31408
                                                                CIP

9 8 7 6 5 4 3 2
First printing

To all CAP Marines, living and dead . . . and to Sue.

Contents

Contents
_____

viii

Foreword

It is commonly contended that the French defeat in the Indochina War (1944–54) began in Paris, caused by inadequate, uncertain, and delayed support for the French Expeditionary Force. In fact, the commanders on the ground were even more responsible for the disaster, because they failed to recognize that Ho Chi Minh had won the loyalty and confidence of 15 million people. No level of French paratroops, tanks, and river boats was likely to alter the situation as long as the French soldiers were unable to capture the trust of the common people. This they failed to do. Indeed, there is little evidence that the French ever perceived the critical importance of popular support. And they lost the war.

There is some analogy to be found between the French defeat and the tragic American outcome in Vietnam. Our leadership, from Washington down, for the most part accorded too little importance to the war among the people and was too willing to address the Vietnam conflict as if it were being fought on the West German Plain.

But this shortcoming was not universal. Almost from the moment of their arrival in Vietnam in 1965, the U.S. Marines emphasized the critical importance of gaining the confidence and support of the people in the 14,000 Vietnamese villages. By their behavior, the Marines sought to persuade the villagers in the northern part of South Vietnam that, while they might look like Frenchmen, they were actually mindful of their problems and could be depended on to help solve them.

This operational emphasis was not accepted with universal enthusiasm throughout our own ranks. The Secretary of Defense declared that the project of changing native minds was understandable but unacceptable because it would consume too much time. The U.S. military commander in Vietnam clung to the belief that destruction of the regular North Vietnamese units was of higher priority. Known as the search-and-destroy mentality, it controlled all that we did. It was in this inhospitable atmosphere that the concept of combined-action teams began.

The first Marines who came to Vietnam learned quickly that the Vietnamese peasant was tired of war, hungry for a little tranquility, and terrified of the Vietcong guerrillas who dominated their lives. They were tired of a life in which the Vietcong murdered village mayors, extracted rice and tribute, labor and information from the villagers and impressed their children into the Vietcong ranks.

All the common people could fall back on for direct protection were local volunteers, the Popular Forces. These were boys from the village, miserably equipped, ill-paid, poorly led, poorly trained, and frightened. They were no match for the hardened Vietcong guerrillas and did not venture out of their houses after dark to oppose them. They had just one thing going for them: they were fighting for their homes, their mothers, their sweethearts.

The Combined Action Program's basic concept was to bring peace to the Vietnamese villages by uniting the local knowledge of the Popular Forces with the professional skill and superior equipment of the Marines. There was about a squad of Marines with a hospital corpsman to a platoon of Popular Forces. The Vietnamese knew who the guerrillas were and where they hid; the Americans knew how to kill them.

Marines had done this sort of thing before—in Haiti, Santo Domingo, and Nicaragua—but never in such a severe combat environment. There is no certain evidence as to who first proposed to bring the combined-action scheme to Vietnam, but Lt. Gen. Lewis W. Walt and I supported it strongly. As time passed, it also acquired support at lower levels.

Hemingway's book illustrates the reality of how such a scheme matures: awkwardly, haltingly, sometimes disappointingly, but always adhering to the fundamental idea. His story is told through the unmetered words of Marines who describe simply what they did and what they saw. There is a ring of truth and a smell of gunsmoke in their declarations. Although very different from one another, the stories also exhibit several ideas in common.

A sense of the soundness of the concept is present throughout the book. The Marines were enthusiastic about the program, and they empathized with the Popular Forces and the villagers whose confidence they sought to win.

The Marines were aware of the high esteem in which the natives held the CAP medical corpsman. Good health was probably so important to the villagers that the person who could bring it to them had a strong call on their loyalty.

Finally, the CAP Marines took great pride in the combat success achieved by many of the platoons. No village captured from the Vietcong was ever retaken, and 60 percent of CAP Marines volunteered to extend their time with the program. This can leave no doubt as to its value.

Beyond its contribution to the history of a war many would like to forget, Hemingway's chronicle has real value for the future. American forces may well be involved in other relatively undeveloped areas. This book can serve as a series of guideposts, with its credible examples of right and wrong in the critical task of winning the support of the people. Without their support, as Vietnam taught us, victory is out of reach.

Victor H. Krulak
Lieutenant General, USMC, Ret.

Preface

Khe Sanh. Hue City. Dewey Canyon. Starlite. Hastings. These are but a few of the battles and campaigns that the United States Marine Corps participated in during its lengthy deployment in South Vietnam.

In addition to their traditional combat role, the Marines were innovators, paradoxically, in another field—pacification. When Marine units arrived in Vietnam in force in March 1965, they began to develop plans to provide security for the villages and hamlets and to permanently oust communist guerrillas operating in their areas. By the summer, the Combined Action Platoons (CAPs) had been introduced to execute these plans.

Little has been written about this unique group in Vietnam. While most Marines just passed through the villes and hamlets within their areas of operation (AOs), the CAPs lived, ate, worked, and fought alongside their Vietnamese counterparts, the Popular and Regional Forces (PFs and RFs). The key to the program was the bond between the Vietnamese and the Americans.

This book is not an official history of the CAPs; rather, it is an intimate look at life in the villages, as experienced by CAP members from different platoons throughout the I Corps section of Vietnam. These young leathernecks had to determine whether or not pacification could be achieved in the villages they were assigned to.

The military and political aspects of the Vietnam conflict have been examined in exhaustive detail, but two books in particular address the Combined Action Program. Francis J. West's *The Village* (1972) covers a specific CAP in a specific area; William R. Corson's *The Betrayal* (1968) deals with the overall pacification effort.

The oral history format I've chosen here includes accounts from CAP Marines who served in different platoons, in a variety of villages, throughout the conflict. The narratives appear in loose chronological order. In the early days CAP Marines were in fixed positions, and their experiences differed considerably from those of the Marines in mobile CAPs toward the end of the war.

Each CAP Marine faced distinct problems in the area he was assigned to. Not all Marines were fond of PFs, for example, nor were they readily accepted by the inhabitants of the village they occupied. A Marine situated in 2d Combined Action Group (CAG), outside of Da Nang, might confront more local insurgents, whereas another Marine, located in 4th CAG in northern Quang Tri Province, might regularly encounter North Vietnamese Army (NVA) units because of the scarcity of villages in that sector.

No other military organization had anything quite like the Marine CAP. The U.S. Army did have a group called the Mobile Advisory Team (MAT) that consisted of two officers, three enlisted men, and an ARVN interpreter. These MAT teams traveled among the villes within a designated area training PFs and RFs. By the end of 1970, nearly five hundred MATS were operational. Special Forces A Teams, composed of twelve Green Berets, were similar to CAPs. However, the A Teams had the advantage of longer stateside training, the presence of officers or senior enlisted men, and additional reinforcements of Montagnards or Chinese Nungs at their campsites.

The pacification effort was a viable alternative to the search-and-destroy mentality touted by the high command in Vietnam. Applied on a larger scale, the Combined Action Program might have achieved greater results. With the apparent demise of the Cold War and the prospect of increased low-intensity conflicts, it is appropriate to ask if a Combined Action Program might be successful in Central or South America, for example.

The experiences of the CAP Marines I interviewed for this book may help to shed some light on this aspect of the Vietnam War. They did an outstanding job. They were thrust into an alien culture to live, work, fight, and—in many cases—die. They are intensely proud of their CAP service in spite of the outcome of the Vietnam War.

Acknowledgments

There are many individuals to whom I am grateful for assisting me in the research, editing, and publishing of this book.

Artie Falco prodded me to write about the CAP Marines over a beer one night (in a bar, where else?) at the Port 5 in Bridgeport, Connecticut. He piqued my interest; the result is this book.

Tom Harvey, editor of the CAP Association newsletter, offered invaluable guidance and suggestions.

Mark Gatlin, acquisitions editor at the Naval Institute Press, offered encouragement and constructive criticism.

Paul Hernandez wrote some of the most beautiful letters I have ever read. He has found an inner peace that most of us spend a lifetime looking for.

Rocky Jay's unique sense of humor got me through some rough spots, and his three-alarm chili with the homegrown jalapeño peppers kept me up nights. We figured out that it could have been me who radioed in his medevac chopper the day he was seriously wounded near Dong Ha on October 5, 1969. God, I hope it was.

Finally, I am grateful to all the CAP Marines who allowed me to interview them for this book. It was difficult for some to relive those moments that have haunted them for so many years.

I salute them.

Semper Fidelis.

Our War Was Different

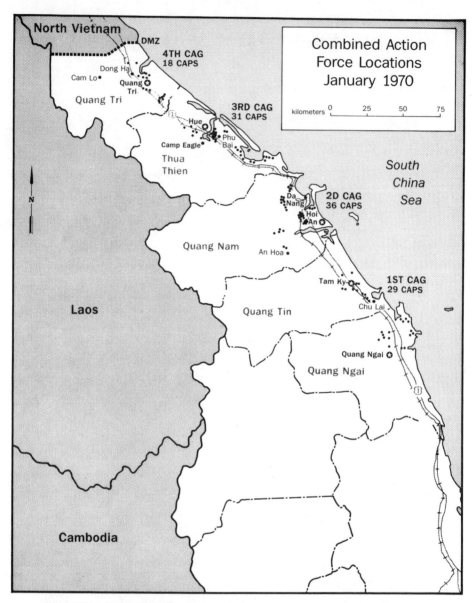

**Combined Action
Force Locations
January 1970**

North Vietnam

DMZ

**4TH CAG
18 CAPS**

Dong Ha
Cam Lo •
Quang ⊙
Tri
Quang Tri

**3RD CAG
31 CAPS**

kilometers 0   25   50   75

Hue ⊙
Camp Eagle •
Phu
Bai
Thua
Thien

South
China
Sea

Da
Nang
Hoi
An ⊙

**2D CAG
36 CAPS**

Quang Nam
An Hoa •

Laos

Tam Ky ⊙

**1ST CAG
29 CAPS**

Chu Lai

Quang Tin

Quang Ngai ⊙
Quang Ngai

Cambodia

MAP BY W. STEPHEN HILL, COURTESY OF THE USMC HISTORICAL CENTER

USMC Combined Action Program: An Overview

The concept underlying the Combined Action Program was not new to the Marine Corps. Similar programs were used during conflicts in Haiti (1915–34), Nicaragua (1926–33), and, most effectively, Santo Domingo (1916–22). During these so-called Banana Wars, U.S. Marines in Nicaragua organized, trained, and directed a new national police force, the Guardia Nacionál, later to become the Policia Nacionál. Legendary Marine Lewis B. "Chesty" Puller attained the rank of captain in the Guard and commanded Company M while serving in the Nicaraguan campaign. He was given the sobriquet El Tigre, the tiger. Rebel leader Augusto Cesar Sandino placed a bounty of 5,000 pesos on Puller's head, dead or alive. (In Vietnam, CAP Marines would also have bounties placed on them.)

During formal training, Policia personnel were imbued with a strong sense of discipline. Under close Marine scrutiny, they exercised their new knowledge and skills by conducting numerous successful antiguerrilla patrols. In the villages, the Marines formed Home Guard units that consisted of one Marine officer, two or three enlisted Marines, and a dozen natives.

The scarcity of combat troops in Vietnam prompted Capt. John J. Mullen, Jr., 3d Battalion, 4th Marines civil affairs officer, to propose an organization comparable to those used in Haiti, Nicaragua, and Santo Domingo before World War II. Plans were soon developed by Maj. Cullen B. Zimmerman, Executive Officer, 3d Battalion, 4th Marines, with the approval of his commanding officer, Lt. Col. William W. Taylor. Operations commenced in the Hue and Phu Bai area on August 3, 1965, with the first platoon led by 1st Lt. Paul Ek. Lt. Gen. Victor H. "Brute" Krulak, Commanding General, Fleet Marine Force, Pacific, and Maj. Gen. Lewis W. Walt, Commanding General, III Marine Amphibious Force (III MAF), gave the project their wholehearted

Lt. Gen. Victor H. "Brute" Krulak

support. The Combined Action Program was born.

During this time the Marines discovered a potential ally in the often belittled and neglected Popular Forces (PFs). The PFs were at the very bottom rung in the Vietnamese military ladder. Usually recruited to serve in their own hamlets and villages, with few exceptions they were incompetent as a fighting force. Ill-equipped, ill-trained, and paid only half of what the regular Army of the Republic of Vietnam (ARVN) soldiers received, the PFs fought indifferently, if at all, and their desertion rate was atrocious. They rarely ventured out at night, and as a result the Viet Cong ruled the countryside during the hours of darkness.

The Marines' scheme was simple. If the PFs could be properly trained in firearms and squad tactics, if they could be instilled with pride and discipline, they just might be transformed into a viable, cohesive unit to augment the CAP Marines in the villes. This was the vital role the CAP Marines were destined to play in Vietnam.

Each CAP consisted of a rifle squad (which was normally understrength because of transfers and rotation), a Navy corpsman, and a thirty-five-man PF or RF platoon. The Marines contributed the air and artillery support; the PFs provided valuable knowledge concerning the terrain and intelligence about Viet Cong (VC) forces operating in the area.

In the summer of 1965, four such CAPs were organized into a Combined Action Company (the acronym CAC was soon changed to CACO because *cac* was found to be a vulgar word in the Vietnamese language). It was originally called a Joint Action Company, but the name was soon changed to indicate that the forces of more than one nation were involved.

The program quickly spread to Da Nang and Chu Lai. By the end of 1966 there were fifty-seven CAPs. Because of the program's rapid growth, III MAF created the Combined Action Groups (CAGs), each with a varied number of companies and each company with a varied number of platoons. By 1970, at the height of the program, there were four CAGs: the 1st CAG near Chu Lai; the 2d CAG near Da Nang; the 3d CAG at Hue and Phu Bai; and the 4th CAG in Northern I Corps in Quang Tri Province. In all there were 42 Marine officers, 2,050 enlisted men, 2 naval officers, and 126 Navy hospital corpsmen in the four CAGs as well as some 3,000 PFs and RFs. The largest group was the 2d CAG in Quang Nam Province; the smallest was the 4th CAG in Quang Tri Province.

Most CAP Marines volunteered from line companies and had at least six months in country. Later in the war some Marines were assigned to CAPs right from the staging battalion at Camp Pendleton, California. These CAP-bound Marines were required to have an above-average general classification test score and a spotless record. The Combined Action Force (CAF) headquarters, formed in January 1970 to consolidate all the CAGs under one command, screened incoming applicants. The usual rejection rate was 20 to 25 percent. Special attention was given to the important position of squad leader, normally given to a sergeant (E-5). However, it was not unusual to find a corporal, or in some instances a lance corporal, leading a CAP.

After being accepted, CAP Marines attended a two-week school in Da Nang before joining their respective units. Classes included refresher training in basic infantry weapons; small-unit tactics; first aid; map and compass reading; war-dog use; procedures for requesting and controlling artillery fire; air strikes; medical evacuation; Vietnamese language, history, and culture; Vietnamese politics; history and organization of the PFs; and VC organization, weapons, and tactics.

It was an arduous two-week schedule. The students also conducted nightly patrols around the CAF compound with local PFs. In January 1966 Gen. Lew Walt expanded the Combined Action Program, and missions were defined in the following manner (Shulimson 1982, 239):

Neutralize the VC threat in the village or hamlet.
Provide security and help maintain law and order.
Protect local Vietnamese authorities.
Guard important facilities and lines of communication within the
village and hamlet.
Conduct combined operations with other allied forces.
Participate in civic-action and psychological operations.
Assist in economic and social development.
Provide military training to the PFs.
Collect intelligence.

The CAPs received orders from their own chain of command: CAG to CACO to CAP. The PFs were, in theory, directly responsible to their village chiefs, but generally they took orders from their district chief, who wielded more power and influence. Located near a province headquarters, each CAG provided administrative support to the CACOs and conferred with province chiefs and unit commanders to allocate the tactical areas of coordination (TAOCs) they would operate in. The CACO headquarters, located at a district headquarters, arranged for artillery and air support, medical evacuation, and reinforcements from the CAP units nearest to them. Operational control of each CAP unit and its PFs rested with the Vietnamese district (subsector) commander. Each specific TAOC was the exclusive territory of the CAP living there, and any other unit had to obtain permission from the CACO and district commanders before penetrating the TAOC. The idea of informing a certain CAP that an infantry unit was entering its AO was sound, because this prevented confusion, but the practice was not always followed. Many times CAP Marines sat silent on a night ambush as a Marine or Army patrol walked through their kill zone never realizing that they were there.

Each CAP was led by a Marine sergeant. A Vietnamese sergeant, or Trung-si, headed the PF platoon. The Marine noncommissioned officer (NCO) and his Vietnamese equivalent consulted on matters pertinent to the village, the inhabitants, and the missions expected of the CAPs. The PFs had no rank structure to speak of and their numbers never exceeded the platoon level, usually between thirty and thirty-five. If a disagreement arose between the two groups, the Marines were supposed to take charge of the situation. Most CAP Marines say that it was difficult to get a platoon of disgruntled PFs to do anything they chose

Col. Edward F. Danowitz, 2d CAG CAP Marines, and PFs with VC weapons captured after action in Hieu Nhon District.

not to do, but usually problems were resolved and the two commands performed remarkably well together.

CAP Marines were almost constantly in the field. As one CAF fact sheet reported, their "classroom was in the 'bush' where the VC provide the necessary training aids" (Smith 1988, 290). During daylight hours some CAP Marines engaged in civic-action projects such as repairing roads, paddy dikes, and schools. The Marines' emphasis was to teach the villagers how to help themselves, but their first priority was combat operations.

Generally the CAP Marines and their Vietnamese counterparts got along, but occasionally there were challenges. Many PFs were reluctant to attend day classes; others had to be coerced into patrolling outside the boundaries of their own ville. The PFs were, however, under extreme pressure from their own village chiefs and the populace to protect them from the ever-present VC threat. Another problem was the possibility of PF cooperation with the enemy.

Before 1969 the CAPs maintained fixed positions in their particular villes. Called compounds, they resembled small triangular-shaped forts. This procedure became costly in terms of casualties, however, because of the defensive mind-set. The fixed compounds

L. Cpl. Paul Hernandez in Thanh Quit with
"Dum-Dum," age eight, November 1970

Children in Cho Mai village

Selling corn at the market in Thanh Quit, March 1968

presented lucrative targets for the enemy, and the threat of being overrun was always imminent. Col. Louis Metzger, later to become Assistant 3d Marine Division Commander, said that "to survive in many CAP TAORs, CAPs had to patrol aggressively" (Cosmas 1986, 145).

Consequently, by mid-1969 mobile CAPs were established. These CAPs set up temporary command posts (CPs) at various locations within their TAORs. At these so-called day havens, the CAP Marines could rest, eat, and clean their weapons while planning the next patrol. While patrolling, the Marines would set up a new CP before nightfall. From this vantage point several fire teams would patrol and set up night ambushes; one of the fire teams would stay behind to guard the CP and maintain radio contact with the others. This mobility enabled the Marines to cover more territory without additional men, and prevented the enemy from knowing the exact whereabouts of the platoon.

By the end of 1969, CAP patrols numbered 145,000, with 73 percent of them at night. CAP Marines initiated two-thirds of

Major General R. V. Tompkins meets with CAG commanders at Da Nang headquarters, October 1968. First row, left to right: Lieutenant Colonel Brady, Tompkins, Colonel Danowitz; second row: Lieutenant Colonels Pierson, Jones, Whitesall, and Greenwood

Village and hamlet chiefs gather with Lieutenant Colonel Greenwood and Colonel Danowitz for a ceremony activating a new CAP in Quang Tri Province, March 1969.

Lt. Gen. Lew Walt (second from left), *assistant commandant of the Marine Corps, visits the 1st Combined Action Group, Chu Lai, October 1968.*

their firefights, which meant they were surprising the enemy by relocating every night. In all, 1,938 enemy were killed, 425 suspected VC agents were captured, and 932 weapons were confiscated.

In less than four years, ninety-three platoons had been transferred from villages deemed safe and ready to undertake their own protective measures. No CAP hamlet ever returned to VC control, according to studies done by the Hamlet Evaluation System, which was established in 1966 to study pertinent data involving pacification. Hamlets were labeled according to their VC presence. There were six categories: A, B, C, D, E, and V. A meant that the hamlet was VC free and V that it was under VC control. There was also a PF platoon evaluation system.

In late 1969 a ticklish question arose. With the 3d Marine Division standing down and readying to redeploy to Okinawa and Hawaii, it was decided to deactivate some of the CAP units. But how would the CAP turn the war over to the villagers?

The organization of the CAGs commenced on February 9, 1970. In March a Civil Operations and Revolutionary Development Support (CORDS) study proposed that the CAPs be "integrated into CORDS." (CORDS had been established in 1967

Combined Action Force headquarters, Da Nang, looking south

to coordinate the pacification programs in South Vietnam.) In essence, they stated that the CAPs duplicated many CORDS functions in the villages. But the Marines argued that the CAPs were involved in combat operations, over which CORDS had no jurisdiction, and at the insistence of the Marines, the idea was scrapped.

Reductions continued through 1970, with the CAF concentrating its forces in Quang Nam Province. By July Marine replacements into the CAPs were at a virtual standstill. Most personnel were shifted to other CAPs or transferred to units leaving Vietnam.

In July 1970 the 4th CAG was deactivated, and on September 7, 1970, 3d CAG Headquarters ceased operations. The following week 1st CAG followed suit. Most of the Marines were reassigned to 2d CAG, which, due to the influx of incoming personnel, blossomed to 650 Marines and 50 Navy corpsmen. By the end of the month the CAF had halted operations.

These were drastic changes, and, according to a 2d CAG operational order dated December 23, 1970, the 2d CAG became the "residual force of the III MAF Combined Action Program" (Cosmas 1986, 151) and established its headquarters at Hoi An, capital of Quang Nam Province. Its mission was to integrate combined-action activities with those of Quang Nam provincial authorities, the 1st Marine Division, and the 2d Republic of Korea (ROK)

Combined Action Force headquarters, Da Nang, looking north

Marine Brigade. Again CORDS endeavored to assert its will by seeking absolute authority over the CAPS, but the attempt failed.

In late 1969 and early 1970, another program was established to augment the CAPs. It was first named the Infantry Company Intensified Pacification Program (ICIPP), but this was changed to Combined Unit Pacification Program (CUPP) in January 1970. Under this concept individual squads from ordinary rifle companies were dispatched to RF or PF platoons in the Marine AO. The Army's Americal Division assigned squads for this duty in October 1969 in Quang Ngai Province, and the 1st Marine Division did likewise around Hill 55 the following month.

Each CUPP squad was tasked with the same nine missions as the CAPs, which continued to operate as before. However, there were two differences: first, CUPP Marines did not attend any formal-type schooling and were not specially trained for their assignment; second, a CUPP squad was not sent outside its AO and remained under operational control of its own regiment. All requests for air, artillery, and medical support were dispatched through each CUPP's regiment.

As the program escalated, every regiment within the 1st Marine Division committed at least one company to the effort. According to Col. John W. Haggerty III, the III MAF's deputy of operations,

One of the kids, 1969

"It's a way to take forces and make [them] much more effective by multiplication . . . without destroying the infantry unit itself. . . . As long as you've got them in a CUPP, you can always bring them back together if you have to" (Cosmas 1986, 155).

The Marine Corps operational units opposed the idea and saw the CUPP as a hindrance, envisioning scenarios in which scattered forces would be vulnerable to attack. However, both III MAF commanders—Lt. Gen. Herman Nickerson, Jr., and his successor, Lt. Gen. Keith B. McCutcheon—embraced the CUPP concept as an excellent asset in the ongoing Vietnamization process started in late 1969.

By the spring of 1970, the 1st Marine Division had twenty-two CUPP squads guarding about 23,000 villagers. To accomplish this, the Marines were conducting operations with sixteen PF and seven RF platoons and the People's Self-Defense Force (PSDF). Most CUPP teams were strung out along routes 1, 4, and 535, or around major allied bases such as Hill 55 and LZ Baldy.

Marines were not placed in a hamlet unless it was classified C or lower by the Hamlet Evaluation System. Once positioned in the hamlets, CUPP units, like the CAPs, spent most of their time patrolling and ambushing. The 1st Marine Division endorsed using mobile CAPs rather than tying down Marines to fixed positions.

Like CAP Marines, the CUPP Marines encouraged RF and PF platoon commanders to plan and lead their own operations. When not actively engaged in these exercises, CUPP units practiced civic action and Medical Civic Action Patrols (MEDCAPs).

Unfortunately, the CUPPs had a serious manpower problem during 1970 and 1971. Many squads, which were supposed to number twelve to fifteen men at full strength, were lucky to have seven or eight. The RFs and PFs suffered the same fate.

For the most part, CUPP morale was not as high as in the CAPs, owing to the low state of proficiency of the RFs and PFs. "You'd look around and . . . there wouldn't be no PFs there," one Marine said. "They'd be hidin' behind gullies, bushes, trees, anything you could find down on the ground . . . you had to knock a few heads . . . put a few rounds over the top of 'em, but they finally got to where they started to go with us."

Despite these setbacks, Marines continued to train the RFs and PFs. Although a slow, plodding process, it did prove, according to one Marine officer, that "they [were] capable of closing with and destroying the local VC."

When the 1st Marine Division returned to the United States in the spring of 1971, the CUPPs were dissolved. The CAP mission was officially terminated after six years of operation.

Sadly, the CAP concept was never fully exploited. One can only speculate on the kind of impact it might have had if it had been allowed, as one high-ranking Marine officer said, "to bear full fruit."

1965–1967

Origins

On March 8, 1965, elements of the 3d Battalion, 9th Marines, landed on Red Beach 2 at Da Nang, South Vietnam. As the infantrymen splashed ashore, leathernecks from the 1st Battalion, 3d Marines were airlifted into the country. The arrival of these two ground combat units heralded the U.S. Marine Corps arrival in South Vietnam.

From the onset, Lt. Gen. Victor H. "Brute" Krulak, Commanding General, Fleet Marine Force, Pacific (FMFPAC) and U.S. Army Gen. William C. Westmoreland, Commanding General, Military Assistance Command, Vietnam (MACV) disagreed about which strategy should be employed to assure success in Vietnam.

Krulak was adamantly opposed to Westmoreland's preferred search-and-destroy approach. Dispatching American troops into the "hinterland," according to Krulak, was a complete waste of time and energy. "Those battles [would be] fought too often on the enemy's terms," he wrote, "where close-quarters combat in the fog-shrouded hills, forests, and vine-thick jungles, with which he was familiar, stretched our logistic system and diminished the effectiveness of U.S. supporting arms, particularly air" (Krulak 1984, 225).

Together with Maj. Gen. Lew Walt, Commanding General, III Marine Amphibious Force (III MAF), Krulak was a proponent of the combined-action approach—Marines and the Vietnamese militia, or Popular Forces (PFs), working hand-in-hand in the villages to deny the enemy recruits, food, and intelligence they needed to achieve victory. Even Gen. Vo Nguyen Giap, commander of the North Vietnamese Army, wrote, "Without the people we have no information. . . . They hide us, protect us, feed us, and tend our wounded" (Krulak 1984, 211).

Despite Westmoreland's objections, the Marines forged ahead with the Combined Action Program. From its modest beginning in 1965, the program did enjoy some early successes. In fact, forty of the sixty-six Marines at Phu Bai from Lt. Paul Ek's original platoons opted to stay instead of returning to their respective units when their tour with CAC was finished.

Encouraged, III MAF wanted to expand the CAPs. From June to December 1966, forty-one new CAPs were established throughout I Corps, bringing the total to fifty-seven. Although this growth was welcome, it also posed some problems, one of which was supplying the CAP Marines. The CAP platoons had to rely on the line battalions operating in their area for supply. Chuck Ratliff, who served with Alpha CAPs in 3d CAG, recalls, "In the early CAPs, we had no parent organization. Whoever moved into Phu Bai, that's who we became attached to."

Not until July 1967, when III MAF Order 3121.4A put the program under direct operational control of III MAF, did the resupply situation begin to improve.

Now that the CAPs had a table of organization and equipment (TO/E) to alleviate the resupply problems, they also acquired a new leader. The program's first director, Lt. Col. William R. Corson, was given the difficult job of reorganizing the fledgling unit. He strongly espoused the combined-action strategy. "Some of our allies," he said, "especially the ones I knew, thought the Combined Action Program was the wisest thing in Vietnam."

During 1966 and 1967, an alarming number of NVA troops streamed into South Vietnam. Marine battalions were sent north and fought a series of pitched battles along the demilitarized zone (DMZ) to stem the communist advance. Some historians argue that the enemy used this strategy to divert attention from the Marines' pacification efforts. General Giap never admitted this, but he alluded to the fact that pacification was curbed because of the NVA buildup in the south. Whether or not his purpose was to prevent or slow pacification remains debatable, but it is certain that the number of CAPs suffered due to the NVA threat. Of the 120 CAPs envisioned by III MAF, about 80 were in place by the end of 1967.

Still, in spite of being hard-pressed for manpower, the Marine Corps blunted the communist invasion and kept the CAPs operational. Whether Westmoreland liked it or not, the Combined Action Program was there to stay.

Comdr. Richard McGonigal, USN (Ret.)

III MAF
1966 – 1969

Richard McGonigal spent three years in Vietnam with the CAP school. He is the only individual to visit every CAP within I Corps. While doing graduate work at Columbia University he was asked by General Krulak to establish a CAP training program and to study which types of Marines and Vietnamese citizens could best work together in a CAP environment. He is a graduate of Cornell University and the Union Seminary in New York City. He also earned his Ph.D. from Michigan State University.

I worked out of III MAF from May 1966 to April 1969 throughout I Corps, surveying the attitudes of Marines, PFs, and ARVN soldiers. I visited and worked with all 114 CAPs.

I went along with the 51st ARVN Regiment on two of their operations. One morning as I watched each ARVN soldier being issued eight rounds of ammo to last for the day, I remember thinking I might have stayed in bed if we had that problem!

I also spent six weeks with the Korean Marines and found examples of incredible courage. They demonstrated the best fire discipline I've ever witnessed. Some were as cruel as hell, but others were sympathetic and excellent on MEDCAPs and civic action.

Was CAP a success? Much of it was geographical. Some units were extremely vulnerable to attack from the NVA; for example the CAP at the base of Marble Mountain had its CP inside the village, right against the Trung-si's house. They figured this way the Trung-si had an extra incentive to keep the VC at a greater grenade-throwing distance from his rack at night.

The CAPs on the other side of the French Fort [3d Marine Division TAOR] were so remote that no one bothered to tell them the division was moving north. The first the CAP knew about it was when the battalion in that area came to get its PRC-25 radio and .50-caliber machine gun. As a result, the CAP had its firepower greatly diminished and was out of touch with everyone else for about a week. No matter how you define success, let's not have it include that kind of "caring for our own."

No question about one thing, though: the CAPs speeded pacification. I felt there was plenty of hardware: tanks, air support, artillery, but the problem was communication and training. It seemed we were always late in getting our support requests to the larger neighboring units. Close air support was very shaky, and usually tardy. Some of us wondered if the support was stronger for units of 100 percent Americans than it was for 50 percent PFs, 50 percent Marines.

Medevacs seemed to work reasonably well with the Vietnamese military, but I don't know how many orphans we created by taking off for a hospital in a helicopter without making arrangements for the parents to know where their child was going.

A few years ago, a group of former CAP Marines and I returned to Vietnam. We were able to locate some of our PFs, and nearly all of them had been "reeducated." But when they saw us (in a bar, where else?), they came right up to us with some of their VC friends whom we'd also known, and their first words were, "Peace . . . you understand? No more war!" A few moments later they were comparing scars and showing pictures of their children and grandchildren.

Khe Sanh, along Route 9, where two CAPs resided, is now an empty clay field with jungle boots strewn around, obviously too big for Vietnamese feet. Stacked in the front yards near the old artillery position at Gio Linh are dozens of undetonated bombs and artillery rounds. Their bright fuses would seem to indicate a special ordnance-disposal operation.

The Vietnamese tried to start a lumber industry, but 20 percent of the trees they harvested were impregnated with shrapnel. They would have had to x-ray all the trees to make sure they were devoid of shrapnel. Otherwise the blades would have shattered on the saws.

I went back to one spit of land near Hoi An where fourteen of our finest CAP leaders were killed. The houses were all rebuilt, water buffalo plowed the rice paddies, and children rode on their backs, just like when we were there. I watched for fish in the farmer's nets. Dysentery was still a visitor and hundreds of graves abounded.

In 1966 I felt the best we could do was limit the carnage. If we chose not to be there, then we would probably develop a holierthan-thou arrogance toward those who did go. But if we went anyway, no matter what others said about us, we would still have our nightmares.

Does any of this constitute success? In war, there can be no success. But if there is ever an occasion, and I think there will be, to try the CAP concept again and do it right, I still think it could work.

★   ★   ★

Commander McGonigal retired from the Navy in 1991. He lives in Carmel Valley, California, where he teaches at the Monterey Institute of International Studies.

Comdr.
Richard
McGonigal

21

Hop Brown

1st Joint Action Company
1965

Originally an infantryman with Company M, 3d Battalion, 4th Marines, Hop Brown later became a member of the first CAP in South Vietnam in August 1965. He developed a strong empathy for the Vietnamese people; he says this is probably because of his experiences while growing up in Harlem.

My first impression upon being assigned to the village of Thuy Luong was one of awe and revulsion. Having grown up in Harlem, I didn't think I'd ever see people living in more squalid and degrading conditions than what I'd left behind.

I served as a rifleman in the 1st Combined Action Company [CAC] at its inception at Phu Bai in August 1965. A squad of thirteen men plus one corpsman was chosen from each company of the 3d Battalion, 4th Marines. I was in M—Mike—Company.

In time my attitude changed toward these people. As I got used to their way of life and started to see their customs and rituals from their point of view, I began to understand that the things I took for granted as an American did not apply to this culture.

My honest opinion of the PFs as a whole is that they joined the local militia unit to avoid actual service in the armed forces of their country. They chose this option to avoid combat and to remain with their families. They weren't well trained, they were ill-equipped, and they lacked the discipline to become an effective fighting force.

This was true for the PF unit I was assigned to, anyway, but after living with them for several months, I began to sympathize with them. I understood their reasons for choosing to remain close to their homes. The VC preyed on the villagers to gain supplies and recruits for their units. They'd come into a village and spout their propaganda, and if the villagers weren't sympathetic toward their cause, they'd forcibly take rice and vegetables as well as young men and women to fill their ranks. They'd seize people

Hop Brown

to perform labor, like digging tunnels and carrying supplies and ammunition, that was necessary to keep their unit functioning. The PFs didn't like to leave their families under the protection of the ARVN units either—they treated the civilians like the VC. They robbed, plundered, and raped the villagers.

The PFs were equipped with the old M-1 carbine, and they only had a few of them to share among themselves. They didn't have flares, bayonets, K-bars [survival knives], canteens, helmets, flak jackets, all the stuff we had. I thought this lack of basic equipment made the PFs' morale very low. Maybe after we arrived in the villages they looked at us and began to think of themselves as less than soldiers or fighting men. I remember them marveling at any new piece of equipment we introduced into our limited arsenal—infrared scopes, claymore mines, listening devices, explosives like composition B and C-4. They didn't know how to maintain their weapons and were amazed that we cleaned ours every day. Then they'd borrow cleaning equipment from us and make some semblance of caring for their weapons.

Before being assigned to a village, all CAC members had to attend classes that lasted three to four weeks. This was an introduction to the Vietnamese language and customs so we could be courteous to the people. Then we expanded our vocabulary and knowledge of the culture and rituals by living with the PFs.

The weather in Vietnam was either hot or wet. The nights during the monsoon season were cold enough, so we wore our field jackets. When it rained during the monsoon season the guys actually took showers in it. I remember being on ambushes and lying in water with only my rifle and head not covered. The heat during the day was so oppressive I couldn't maintain water discipline. I'd be on patrol and drink two canteens of water in two hours. Sometimes we got brief relief by swimming in small streams and rivers with all our clothes on while some guys stood guard. But then the sun would have us completely dry in a matter of minutes.

We operated mostly around the village, which was surrounded by rice paddies, but we also went into the mountains and surrounding jungles. The mountains were hot and the going very hard, climbing up during the day and then setting up an ambush at the top at night. The jungle was mysterious. I could never get comfortable. If we went there overnight I wouldn't sleep. I was petrified of the snakes, monkeys, tigers, leeches, and other wildlife.

The Marines I served with were a very homogeneous group of guys, and there was none of the racial prejudice that was common back in the world. We all judged each other on our own merits rather than the color of our skins.

Of the guys I remember best, the first to come to mind is Hendricks. Even though he was white and I was black, we were the best of friends. We confided in each other, shared our hopes and dreams, talked about our girls and our families. He decided to extend his tour, but I decided to return to the world. We wrote to each other for a while and then we lost contact.

Then there was Pippin, a black guy out of Chicago who served as one of the squad's automatic riflemen. He was a real fun guy, always joking and a pleasure to be with. We always argued about the merits of our respective hometowns. I'd tell him how much better New York was over Chicago and then we'd get into a heated debate.

There was also Henchin, known affectionately as Momma Henchin. He was a black guy from Los Angeles who served as cook for the squad. He was very versatile in preparing C-rations. He combined them with rice and vegetables from the village market.

The only individual I hated was our squad leader. He was a coward, a cheat, and a liar. I know for a fact that he got the Purple Heart for a self-inflicted wound and that he got a Bronze Star that should rightfully have gone to me and a guy named Taylor. This happened one night on ambush. It was learned that the VC were floating down the river under cover of darkness with supplies tied to tree logs. Well, Taylor and I were the rear guard for this particular ambush and when the VC were spotted the enemy was well past the ambush site. We were ordered to run to the other side of the bend to intercept them, and when we got there the logs were going by. We emptied two magazines apiece at these logs. The rest of the squad did open fire on them too, but they were well past the ambush site.

I cannot honestly say that I saw anyone on those logs in the darkness or that it was my fire that killed anyone, but the next morning we got a report that the ARVN had picked up three dead

VC out of the river. A few months later, back in base camp for one of our paydays, I just happened to notice an award ceremony taking place with my squad leader and a Hawaiian corporal being awarded the Bronze Star for that particular action. I felt this was unfair to me, Taylor, and the rest of the squad.

During my tour of duty with the CAC we came into contact with no hard-core NVA units, and almost no VC. I felt they were ill-equipped and ill-trained. We never engaged a VC unit larger than a platoon—they seemed to be a bunch of farmers who picked up rifles at night to fight for a cause they believed in. Some of their weapons were World War I vintage. They lacked discipline; for example they didn't move in a military manner, they talked while moving at night, smoked cigarettes, and didn't know what to do when caught in an ambush. When a VC sniper shot at you, he gave away his position by trying to run.

But on the whole I respected the VC, for their ingenuity, their beliefs, and for their willingness to suffer undue hardships and die for a cause they believed to be just.

I could never understand how they kept getting away from us when we had them cornered in what we thought was an escape-proof trap. The tunnels and spider holes they used to escape and conceal themselves in were beyond my imagination at the time. They fought hard. I don't know what was in their indoctrination and propaganda classes, but it sure gave them incentive to fight and die.

Upon reflection I feel that the South Vietnamese government helped the CAC program, to a certain extent. They supported us by providing intelligence and artillery support, and they made the local village police chief available to us to overcome any problems that came up in the village.

The police chief and village head were instrumental in getting the people to trust us and give us what help we needed in adapting to life in the village. They provided us with materials and labor to help us build a house of bamboo. They didn't overcharge us for food in the marketplace and they made us feel welcome. After a while, when the villagers trusted us, they'd provide us with information about VC movement and suspected VC presence in the village and surrounding areas. I think the South Vietnamese government was grateful for the program because our presence in the villages denied the VC their support, manpower, and safe havens.

As for my unit, I feel that the Marine Corps gave us the support we needed to maintain our existence as an effective unit to do the job that was expected of us. At the beginning, this major told us that if we were hit at night by a superior force, he wouldn't send reinforcements. When we asked what we were supposed to do, he said, "Fight like hell and bring back your dead and wounded." I don't remember what capacity he served in at the CAC or whether he was transferred later, but the first time we called for help at night reinforcements were there, tanks and everything!

The Marine Corps pretty much let us run our own show. We were the first outfit to be allowed to wear camouflage fatigues and even black VC pajamas on our ops. We could also follow up on our own intelligence and do what we felt was right to protect the villagers and win them over to our side.

However, from a personal point of view, the Marine Corps did not give me their full support. I, like the rest of the guys in the 1st CAC, did not volunteer for this duty—we were chosen. What criteria was used in the selection process is a mystery to me, but I think my company commander and platoon commander wanted to get rid of me. I was not what you call a gung-ho Marine. I had a hard time taking orders and putting up with the racial slurs and innuendoes that were prevalent in the Marine Corps at that time. And my rebuttals were not always verbal. I kept just on this side of the line from going to the brig, but I let my presence be known.

After my induction into the CAC, my attitude toward the Marine Corps and my duty changed. I felt I became what was known as a good Marine, but no one gave me the recognition for the job I was doing. For example, on most patrols and ambushes I was the point man; I guess I walked point seven out of ten times. When I complained about it and asked why, the same person who cheated me out of the Bronze Star said, "You know the area better than anyone else, and you don't show up in the dark very easy," or words to that effect. I was a private first class for three and a half years. I did do things back in the world that didn't warrant my being promoted, but my service and conduct in Vietnam were impeccable.

My son was born in October 1965, and when I requested an overseas phone call I was refused, even though I knew it was common practice.

The only bad experience I had in the Combined Action Program was with my squad leader, and the best one was making friends with a young Vietnamese boy. He was different from the other kids in the village because his parents owned a store that the PFs used as their headquarters. He seemed fascinated with my dark skin, and he'd deliver beer to us on his bike. I looked forward to his visits, and I learned Vietnamese phrases from him and taught him English. I think he was twelve. He had a sister, about nineteen, very pretty. I used to tease him about her and he actually tried to get her to talk to me, but she was a cultured Vietnamese woman and refused. Her name was Chanh, Co Chanh. The day I left his whole family came to say good-bye to me. I was very touched by the affection that was shown to me.

I would say, without trying to be biased, that the Combined Action Program was very successful. Through our commitment we demonstrated to the Vietnamese people that they could trust us. I think living in the villages, amongst the people, we showed them that we could face the same dangers they did. We didn't abuse them or their women, either physically or verbally. We honored their customs and traditions.

I also believe that the Combined Action Program was a growth process for the men who were fortunate enough to participate in it. We developed a camaraderie that was unlike anything I felt while with a company or platoon. We were more of a family than a multi-ethnic fighting unit, and we learned from each other. We expressed our fears and doubts to each other.

I understand that the units involved were given a Presidential Unit Citation and Vietnamese Cross of Gallantry.

I am an incarcerated vet, and must devote most of my time to doing law work in an effort to prove my innocence and be released from prison. I haven't seen or been in touch with members of my squad from the 1st CAC since leaving Vietnam. Maybe they're ashamed of those of us who didn't make it upon our return.

★   ★   ★

Hubert "Hop" Brown is currently an inmate at the Eastern New York Correctional Facility in Napanoch, New York, where he is serving time for substance-abuse charges.

Chuck Ratliff

3d CAG
1966–1967

Before being transferred to a CAP unit, Chuck Ratliff was a rifleman with Company G, 2d Battalion, 1st Marine Regiment. He spent eighteen months in South Vietnam, most of that time with Alpha CAPs near Phu Bai.

I went into the CAC units in May 1966. My first was Alpha-1, situated north of the Phu Bai landing strip. The village was Cho Luong Van.

Alpha-1 consisted of about ten Marines commanded by Sgt. John McKay. Most of these people had participated in Operations Starlite and Harvest Moon. Our job was basically to win the hearts and minds of the people and protect the village.

Probably the most popular person in Alpha-1 was our Navy corpsman. He'd hold sick call for the villagers, and sometimes over a hundred peasants showed up. He'd show the kids and their parents how to wash and treat minor cases, and if anyone needed more, he'd make arrangements for them to be transported to Phu Bai Hospital. You won't find too many Marines that'll dispute the fact that Doc won more hearts and minds than all of us combined.

We saw very little combat at Alpha-1. We'd be used as a blocking force sometimes, but no real action. So we had quite a bit of time to mingle with the people. I went to weddings, people's houses, even a few parties. I adopted a kid named Thi. I made a cot for him and he slept in our compound. In the morning I'd wake him up, feed him C-rations, and send him off to school, which was about a hundred yards south of the compound. We paid a mama-san to do our laundry.

Occasionally we visited a Catholic orphanage in our TAOR. All the kids had lost their parents. Some fought for the North and some for the South.

In the early CACs we had no parent organization. Whoever moved into Phu Bai, that's who we became attached to. My mailing address changed every sixty days or so. I was attached to 1/4, 2/4, 3/4, 1/9, and 2/9 [1st Battalion, 4th Marines; 2d Battalion, 4th Marines; 3d Battalion, 4th Marines; 1st Battalion, 9th Marines; and 2d Battalion, 9th Marines], without ever leaving the compound. It looked as if nobody wanted us.

I extended my tour to stay with the CAC, and after my thirty-day leave I was told I was being transferred to Alpha 6-9.

Of all the CACs, Alpha 6-9 saw the most action. They took the 6th and 9th squads and combined them and they shared the same compound. There were about twenty Marines and twenty PFs. Our assignment was to protect the hamlet of Thon Thuong Lam, and a small portion of Highway 1 between Phu Bai and Hue City, from VC activity.

The senior Marine in the CAP and I had the same last name. Sgt. Dallas Ratliff had eight years in the Corps; he used to say he'd stay in the Corps as long as it would have him. Since I loved the Marine Corps about as much as Sergeant Ratliff, we became friends. He was a good Marine. When I first arrived at Alpha 6-9, he asked me who I'd pissed off. I said I hadn't pissed off anybody that I was aware of. He said I must have. It was the only way anyone got in Alpha 6-9.

At that time the normal Marine squad had thirteen men, but because of a manpower shortage, we had what we called short squads in the CAP. These short squads were made up of six or seven Marines.

I was a nineteen-year-old corporal and leader of the 3d squad. My squad was *real* short—only five men. Cpl. Frank Garcia, the senior Marine, had been squad leader before me. The others were Lance Corporal Baker from somewhere in Oklahoma, Private First Class Johnson from up north somewhere, and Lance Corporal Klipple from parts unknown. Baker was a funny guy, he laughed even in the hardest of times. Klipple never said much but was always friendly and easy to work with. Johnson liked to talk back but never caused any trouble. All of them were good Marines who knew what to do when we made contact with the enemy. I always felt secure around them and was proud of them. Every one of my men had been in combat and had passed the test. We could leave the compound on a night patrol and never touch a trail except to cross from one side to the other. We learned to move together as if we were one, and we never made a sound. We were among the best at what we did.

Squads in CAP Alpha 6-9 rotated from patrolling to bunker

Chuck Ratliff

watch to compound maintenance. The unit normally ran two daytime patrols and one night combat patrol.

August 4, 1967, was my squad's day to run patrols. Marine patrols from CAP Alpha 6-9 had been out all night, and those who hadn't gone out had spent the night on bunker or radio watch. No one had gotten much sleep, but that was normal.

The day patrols were routine, each one about four to five hours. The purpose of these daytime recon patrols was to gather information about the enemy from the people and to make ourselves visible to the general population. Sometimes we visited a local hospital or maybe spent a few hours in the marketplace. The patrols were generally fun because we got to meet the Vietnamese people and we very seldom made contact with the enemy. But nighttime combat patrol was very different. Then we were looking for the enemy, and we felt some degree of failure if we couldn't find him. These patrols could be dangerous and very tense—they drained you emotionally.

As we prepared for our night patrol, I decided to leave Baker behind. He was due to go home shortly and he was extremely upset because his orders back to the "world" had been delayed. This left myself, Garcia, Klipple, Johnson, Doc, our Navy corpsman, and three PFs. We conducted our patrol briefing so everyone could receive their assignments and order of march. We covered things like who would run point and who would carry water and extra ammo.

We left the compound at about 6:30 P.M. in order to arrive at our ambush site by 7:30 P.M. I took the point. The rest of the patrol was staggered—Marine, PF, Marine, PF, and so on. Doc was in the middle of the pack and Johnson was carrying the radio.

This was one of my first patrols with the M-16 rifle. We were real pleased we could carry so much more ammo. I was able to carry 500 rounds myself. But at the same time we were concerned because we'd heard it didn't hold up under combat conditions in the jungle. Garcia and Doc also had M-16s. Johnson had the M-79 grenade launcher and Klipple humped the M-60 machine gun.

It was dusk when we finally reached our location, and I halted the patrol along the edge of this trail about thirty meters from the ambush site, so I could look the terrain over before we moved in. I motioned for Garcia to join me and help recon the area.

As I was looking back at the rest of the patrol, I noticed that one of the PFs seemed to be aiming his rifle right at my head. As he fired, I heard the bullet whiz past my head in slow motion. I thought he was shooting at me. As the round went by I looked the other way. I saw a VC soldier dressed in black falling to the ground with a bullet hole in his forehead. I only saw him for a few seconds but to this day I can still picture his face in my mind. The PF had seen this VC sneak up on me and didn't have time to warn me, so he shot him.

The next fifteen minutes seemed like a lifetime. Bullets tore up the grass all around us as we started to draw fire from a tree line about twenty yards away. Grenades were going off and people were yelling and screaming. I fired my M-16 on full automatic and it jammed after five rounds. I cleared it and fired again, but this time it jammed after only a few rounds.

Klipple went down with a head wound and Doc and I ran over to him. As I lifted his head I could feel his brains in my hand. I told him he was going to be alright and not to go to sleep.

Johnson scurried over and grabbed Klipple's M-60 while I took the M-79, but a few seconds later Johnson was struck in the head. I was lying next to him firing my blooper and saying it didn't look bad. But I was thinking he'd never make it.

By this time the VC were closing in and we were within a few yards of each other. I fired my M-79 into a VC just a few feet from me. The round didn't explode because it hadn't traveled far enough to arm itself. I picked up the M-60 that Johnson had and let loose some bursts at the brush in front of me where I could see muzzle flashes. Then the M-60 jammed, but I was able to clear it and continue firing.

Then there was a flash and a loud bang next to me. I fell to the ground and felt warm blood running down my left arm but I didn't feel any pain. I yelled, "Doc, I'm hit! No, I don't think I am . . . yes . . . I am! Get me some help!"

Just then I heard Garcia holler. He said he'd broken through their lines and was going to circle the VC. He told me to stay where I was because there were too many of them. Garcia and I were the only ones left. Doc was giving first aid to Klipple and Johnson, and the PFs had left the area.

As Garcia was advancing, a second grenade went off near me. I fell to the ground again but, just like before, I felt no pain. I got on my feet and suddenly everything turned real quiet. It seemed to be finished.

A few minutes later a CAP reaction force arrived on the scene. Doc and I prepared Johnson and Klipple for medevac, and we found Garcia not ten meters in front of my position. He'd sustained several wounds and was bleeding heavily, but he was still alive.

The next morning a general arrived at our compound. Word had reached headquarters about our M-16s jamming, so they wanted to inspect them. We were ordered not to let anyone touch the rifles until they were inspected. The first thing he said was, "No wonder they didn't work, look how dirty they are!"

When we tried to explain that the weapons had been cleaned before the patrol and the dirt was from the firefight, he got angry and told us not to get smart with him. This was one of the few times I have ever seen a Marine Corps officer make a total ass of himself.

Later we learned that Garcia died. I saw quite a few men die in Vietnam but Garcia's death was particularly hard. He was such a good person.

Klipple and Johnson were seriously wounded but alive. Two days later the first sergeant asked me to accompany him to Phu Bai and identify Garcia's body. After that we went to see Klipple, who didn't know who I was or where he was. His head had been shaved and you could see where they'd opened him up. The doctors said he was lucky, but he didn't look very lucky to me.

I never found out where they took Johnson. I never saw him again.

This was a bad time for CAP Alpha 6-9. We had lost three excellent Marines. And here's the irony of Vietnam: to this day I don't remember Johnson's or Klipple's first names. I may not even have Klipple's name spelled right. And I have no idea what Doc's name was. I think most Vietnam vets can relate to that.

However, I do know that these people did an above-average job when their country called them. I'm not sure Frank Garcia ever got a medal for his outstanding performance the night he lost his life. I did put in a request that he be decorated, but I was told that an officer had to witness the act. We didn't have officers in the CAP units, so I don't know what ever became of that recommendation.

On September 11, 1967, Sgt. Dallas Ratliff lost his life, hit in the chest by a B-40 rocket as CAP Alpha 6-9's compound was overrun by a VC unit.

I left Alpha 6-9 in October 1967. I entered as a private first class and came out a sergeant. After I left, they finally made it a regular unit recognized by the Marine Corps. Nobody except a few really understood what our job was. Col. Bill Corson, the first director, was very instrumental in the program and always supported us—he knew what we were about.

In November 1986 I found out that the rest of CAP Alpha 6-9 was lost during the 1968 Tet Offensive. I was told they went down fighting in an attempt to hold Highway I, trying to stop the NVA from reaching Hue City so the Marines could move in.

That's why they were there.

★　　★　　★

Since 1974, Chuck Ratliff has been a police officer with the Duncanville Police Department in Duncanville, Texas.

Maj. Edward Palm, USMC (Ret.)

3d CAG
1967

Describing himself as a rear-echelon Marine, Major Edward Palm, then a corporal, got into the program when the Marine Corps expanded and consolidated it in early 1967. He was assigned to Tiger Papa Three in Northern I Corps, where he later became a patrol leader.

I enlisted in the Marine Corps in August 1965, the summer after my graduation from the Salesianum School for Boys, a private Catholic high school in Wilmington, Delaware. I was a corporal and had no college whatsoever when I reported to Vietnam in November 1966.

I served as a patrol leader with the 3d platoon of Papa Company [Papa Three], 3d Combined Action Group. Papa Three lived and operated in a village complex called Thon Vinh Dai, adjacent to Route 9, about halfway between Dong Ha and Cam Lo in Quang Tri Province [South Vietnam's northernmost area]. None of us knew the name of the village at the time; it didn't seem important.

The terrain to our north was largely flat, consisting of rice paddies and wooded areas. There were small hamlets throughout the area, and to the south were rolling hills and small ravines covered with scrub brush. The dominant geographic feature in our TAOR was the Song Cam Lo, an unfordable river we could cross only by boat. Monsoon nights could seem brutally cold, particularly when you were wet and the wind was blowing. We were far enough north that the heat was bearable; at least I don't remember being uncomfortably hot at Papa Three, and I remember the early fall as cool and pleasant.

A typical patrol began with Sarge, our squad leader, briefing the Trung-si the day before. Sarge showed him an overlay and requested that a number of PFs, usually twelve, be ready at the appointed time and place. If four or five showed up we were lucky. Despite numerous suggestions, complaints, and threats, we were never able to form integrated, cohesive patrolling teams. It was the luck of the draw every time out.

Once in the field the PFs generally followed our lead, so long as we were patrolling our own side of the river. We had patrolled the other side together on several occasions, without incident and without complaint, so it came as a complete surprise one day when they simply staged a sit-down strike at the river's edge and refused to budge. They said there were "beaucoup VC" on the other side of the river. We tried, but we never could get the PFs to see this as an opportunity, and we eventually broke with them over this and another issue: an Air Force gunship, nicknamed Puff the Magic Dragon, mistook us one night for the enemy and lightly wounded two Marines but killed two PFs and wounded another. The PFs blamed us, and by late fall of 1967 Papa Three Marines and PFs were patrolling separately.

Day patrols were see-and-be-seen operations, uneventful walks around the hamlets to demonstrate our presence. Night ambushes usually left after dark and remained in the ambush site until dawn. All our patrols, except for one, were uneventful. On that occasion no PFs were present. They were still sitting it out over Puff and our insistence on patrolling the far side of the river.

It was December 4, 1967. Six Papa Three Marines set out that morning; I was not one of them. We'd formed into two teams, and my team had the ambush patrol that night. It was the other team's turn to run the day patrol.

The day patrol's mission was to check out the remotest corner of our area, a small hamlet on the other side of the river 2,000 meters out. It was a cool and balmy day and the sun was shining, which probably contributed to the patrol's complacency. The warning signs were there: no matter what time of day Papa Three came through this particular hamlet it seemed strangely deserted, as if the people had just left. When we did find people there were no males of military age, just old men and women.

Papa Three had carelessly set a pattern, taking a break in the same deserted hootch every time it patrolled this hamlet. Finally the enemy capitalized on the mistake; they allowed the patrol to relax and then opened fire from a tree line not more than fifty yards away. Miraculously, only one man, L. Cpl. James L. Reaves, was hit in the initial burst—in the hand. He was able to speak to another Marine, but shortly thereafter he was struck in the head and died instantly. The others found cover in a root cellar.

Cpl. Edward Palm on patrol (left)

The NVA also made a mistake, fortunately. They stood off in the tree line and failed to close in on the trapped Marines, and the radio operator who'd saved us several days earlier, with his coolness under friendly fire from Puff the Magic Dragon, repeated his performance. Two helicopter gunships were there within minutes. The choppers later claimed six confirmed and five probable kills, but no bodies were found. Four members of the patrol were wounded, two seriously, and Reaves was dead.

While returning to the compound, the rescued patrol captured two VC who were trying to hide in a rice paddy. Later I helped guard them as an interrogation team questioned them. One remained stoically silent, but the other wept and talked eagerly. They were members of a VC main-force psychological operations company attached to a local VC unit. They were competing with us to win the hearts and minds of the people.

We were bitter at our supposed allies for not being on the patrol. They were out on a "PF-only operation" at the time, or so they claimed. But that was overshadowed by another concern. For the Marine Corps at least, these were the early days of the M-16 rifle—every rifle carried by the Marines on that patrol had jammed when it was needed most. One irate Marine threw his on the ground and called it a piece of shit. We watched in awe as another Marine test-fired an AK-47 he found that day; it was caked with mud. He made sure the chamber and barrel were clear and proceeded to empty a thirty-round banana clip without a stoppage.

One grisly task remained—identifying Reaves's body. I volunteered. I felt it was the least I could do, having missed the patrol by a quirk of fate. The company gunnery sergeant and I rode several miles to Dong Ha [3d Marine Division Headquarters] in a jeep.

We were directed to a small unmarked shack that we were told was Graves Registration. It was the most macabre scene I've ever witnessed. I felt like it was a cottage-industry of death. We found ourselves in a room with six preparation tables: two-by-fours and sheets of corrugated tin. The floor was concrete and had recently been hosed down; three naked bodies were laid out in plain view.

A Marine attendant led me into a narrow back room where Reaves was laid out. This room was equipped with the sort of stainless-steel drawers you see in TV and movie morgue scenes. My guide pulled out one of the lower drawers, and it extended the entire length of the room, touching the opposite wall. The body was encased in a translucent, zippered plastic bag, which the Marine unzipped. I recognized Reaves at a glance, but before I could go my ghoulish guide insisted on tilting the head, first one way then the other, to show the gaping exit wound on one side. I was too shaken to concentrate when the attendant asked me to count and sign a receipt for $300 found on Reaves's body. On the way back to our ville the gunny said, "Hell of a way to make a living, isn't it, Palm?" I agreed, and not another word was spoken all the way back to Papa Three.

There was nothing to do but resume our routine. We were still alienated from the PFs, and we hadn't reconciled when I rotated back to the world in early January 1968. I judged PFs quite harshly then, but knowing what I know now I can hardly blame them for their reluctance to fight the war. They stayed in the compound, on average, only one night out of three. The rest of the time they were on their own, living among VC and VC sympathizers. At least one village official was assassinated during my time with the program. Also, the Saigon government, built out of the remnants of the old French civil service, must have seemed as alien to them as we were. Thon Vinh Dai was a traditional Vietnamese village out in the countryside, where western ideas and influences hadn't taken hold, and abstract ideas like democracy and freedom didn't mean much to our PFs. I believe they really didn't see themselves as able to alter the course of events or sway the outcome. The best they could do was get on the winning side and hope for the best.

Failing that, they could only hope to stay out of the war's way.

The village seemed aloof, intent on ignoring our presence. That was my first impression, and nothing happened to change it during my six months with Papa Three. An occasional villager would seek minor medical attention from our corpsman, but the attitude seemed to be mostly cold indifference verging on hostility. Our PFs were standoffish, mostly, and they associated with us only when they had to.

I saw no evidence of direct obstruction on the part of the South Vietnamese government toward the Combined Action Program, but I didn't see any enthusiastic support, either. We tried to operate the program on the basis of a loose alliance, but we should have been a unified command with authority over the PFs. The South Vietnamese government seemed satisfied to let us fight the war while they worried about protecting their position as the ruling elite. I think they gave only token support to the Combined Action Program, at least in our area, and they were certainly an alien presence to the local people.

As I look back on Papa Three today, I realize that what we really needed was greater supervision, but at the time we saw ourselves as suffering most in the areas of supply and logistics.

Early that fall Papa Three had been through a devastating flood, and were demoralized. We had to rebuild our compound from scratch on higher ground, and we weren't making much headway. Then one day we got lucky. *The* senior Marine in Vietnam—Lt. Gen. Robert E. Cushman, Jr.—just happened to be riding by in a jeep when he spotted us. We were a ragtag-looking bunch, filling sandbags on the top of a hill in the middle of nowhere. Out of idle curiosity, probably, he drove to the top of our hill, stopped the jeep, and sauntered over. We overcame our shock at the sight of his three stars and identified ourselves. He immediately pulled up a sandbag and sat down, inviting us to tell him about our unit and our problems. We told him about the flood and the shortages of food and building supplies; we complained that the PFs weren't patrolling with us and weren't pitching in with the rebuilding. In general, we portrayed ourselves as orphans of the storm.

He said he would see what he could do for us, and about a week later a detachment of Seabees arrived. Within a week, Papa Three had a new hilltop encampment complete with a defensive trench, two hardback hootches, and an outhouse. The future Commandant of the Marine Corps had kept his promise to help us.

I am still amazed at the incredible discipline and patience of the NVA and the VC. I don't think they were supermen, as some do. They made mistakes, and several Papa Three Marines owe their survival on December 4, 1967, to one of those mistakes. But they were capable of biding their time, and they didn't jeopardize preparations for the coming 1968 Tet Offensive.

I don't know about attributing great success to the CAP program in general. As I wrote in "Tiger Papa Three" [*Marine Corps Gazette*, Jan. 1988, 34–43; Feb. 1988, 66–76], I know many CAPs fared better than Papa Three, and many fared much worse. My article talks about the difficulty of really knowing what was going on in a Vietnamese village. Because of the cultural and language barriers, I suspect many CAPs only appeared successful. I also suspect that where the program *seemed* most successful was where there'd been a western influence since the French years. I think that maybe where combined action was most needed, out in the VC strongholds, it suited the other side's purpose to tolerate it. Anyway, I don't think combined action could ever have worked well enough to make a difference.

Still, as a gesture of dissent against a failing search-and-destroy strategy, the Combined Action Program was a noble, enlightened effort. The Marine Corps deserves high praise for at least recognizing that we couldn't win that kind of war without winning the allegiance of the people. But I don't think we could ever have found enough Marines with the intelligence and sensitivity to make it work on a large scale, nor could we have provided the language and cultural training. And if the program was so successful, why didn't it turn up any hard intelligence of the Tet Offensive?

An Army colleague of mine once said of the post-Vietnam military mentality, "It's okay to be a Vietnam veteran, so long as you don't dwell on it or refer back to it." I think we're finally outgrowing that attitude, but we seem to have regressed with the euphoria of the Gulf War. The Gulf War doesn't exorcise the ghost of Vietnam. To borrow Hamlet's phrase, it's "an honest ghost" with much to tell about who we are as a nation.

I believe that Vietnam was a tragic mistake for our country, but I've never regretted my own service there. It was the big event of my generation, and those of us who served with the Combined Action Program had a unique vantage point. My only regret is that I didn't extend my tour. I rotated in early January 1968, and

I've never been able to learn how Papa Three fared during the Tet Offensive. I still feel guilty about leaving when I did and also about missing that patrol on December 4, 1967.

★ ★ ★

An assistant professor of English at the U.S. Naval Academy in Annapolis, Maryland, Maj. Edward Palm retired in 1993. His article "Tiger Papa Three" won the 1989 Colonel Robert D. Heinl, Jr., Memorial Award for Marine Corps History.

Tony Vieira

1st CAG
1967–1968

Tony Vieira reenlisted in the Marine Corps to volunteer for duty in Vietnam, where he served nineteen months with Kilo and Lima CAPs in the Chu Lai area.

My first time in the Marine Corps was from August 1959 till 1963. I reenlisted in February 1967 to do my part in Vietnam. I just couldn't sit at home watching the war on TV, not doing my part. I had to go back in.

I served two tours in Vietnam, nineteen months with four different CAPs: Kilo-3, Kilo-4, Lima-7, and Lima-5. All of them were about twenty to twenty-five miles south of Chu Lai—not far from My Lai, or what we called Pinkville.

The only thing I remember about CAP school in Da Nang was they taught us how to play Chinese checkers. I guess they figured it would help us get along with the Vietnamese.

But when you get twelve Marines and a Navy corpsman out in the bush with nobody to depend on but yourselves, you learn real quick.

We had several Army units in our AO who we operated with. The 196th Light Infantry Brigade was a pretty good outfit, real professional. But the 198th Light Infantry Brigade wasn't, so we kept our distance as much as possible.

Most of the PFs I saw were useless; there were only a few that would stand toe-to-toe with you if the shit hit the fan. Most of them only cared about liberty call. They went to the village and goofed off. Then if any kind of serious situation did occur, they ran to us to take charge, which we always did.

The South Vietnamese government was thoroughly corrupt, but the district and province chiefs really liked us. If a CAP was in their area, it was somewhat secure at least. The villagers had no idea what was going on in Saigon and they really didn't care. All they cared about was not being a casualty of the war. You could

Tony Vieira (right)

even be a casualty of voting procedures. They were told who to vote for; it was all fixed. If the villagers didn't vote for the guy the higher-ups wanted, they'd be killed.

I didn't like the fact that we had to pay cash for any mines or booby traps brought in to us. We found out later that the PFs were making their own booby traps and giving them to the kids to bring to us. Paying for booby traps was wrong, as far as I was concerned. It was their war and their country—we were there just to help them.

The Marines gave us as much support as they could. The turn-around point for the approach to Chu Lai Air Base was directly over our TAOR, and when an aircraft went out to dump ordnance at sea, it had to fly over us. The pilot always looked to see if we were in trouble. If it looked like we were, he'd drop that ordnance for us, free of charge. Air power was great!

As far as supplies and weapons went, we took anything that belonged to the Army—M-16s, M-79s, PRC-25s, 60-mm mortars. We even took apart a .50-caliber machine gun piece by piece and brought it to our compound. When the old man came out to visit us he never asked questions. He wouldn't have gotten any answers anyway. We didn't want for anything.

The CAPs never received much coverage, at least ours didn't. We did have several people come out to one of the Lima CAPs when I was there. They snapped a few pictures, asked a few questions, and stayed in the rear drinking beer and chasing girls around before the sun set. But not seeing reporters and photographers was fine with us; all they wanted us to do was play John Wayne for the camera.

I really admired the NVA and the VC. You had to. I hate to say it, but it's true. The Americans had the best of everything—air power, naval gunfire, medical treatment, you name it—and the VC still won. If the ARVNs had half the guts they had, they'd probably still have a country. But the NVA and VC kicked our butts and ran us out of town.

CAP Marines were real close, for the most part. It was like a brotherhood: if you didn't stick together they'd bag you, tag you, and ship you back home. Case closed. I was an E-4 CAP leader with no officers or rear-echelon pogues in my case. They left us alone. We got air strikes, arty, naval gunfire, or whatever on the word of a corporal or a sergeant. Very few units in Vietnam can make that statement. We did basically the same job as the Army Green Berets, with a lot less men and material.

We had an outstanding CO, Colonel Pearson. A real Marine's Marine. Our lieutenant and gunnery sergeant were great too, both killed leading a reactionary force [standby force used to aid other CAPs] into a hot area attempting to save a CAP in trouble. I have tremendous admiration and respect for both of them.

The NVA and the VC hated CAP units because of the damage we did to them. We fought the war on their level and got good results. Every CAP leader, and most of the CAP for that matter, had a bounty on his head, put there by the enemy in an effort to slow us down. But it didn't work.

While I was in the CAP I had both my eardrums blown out by a mortar round. Then when I got home I had to fight like hell to get a service-connected disability from the VA. I don't like the VA. And I don't like the way we were treated when we got home. I think if we'd had the support of our government and the people back home, we could've won that war hands down.

★   ★   ★

After his discharge from the Marine Corps, Tony Vieira served ten years with the Bristol County Sheriff's Department in New Bedford, Massachusetts. He is now retired and lives in Florida.

Jimmy Sparrow

1st CAG
1967

Achieving his childhood dream of becoming a Marine, Connecticut native Jimmy Sparrow arrived in Vietnam in December 1966. He was attached to 1st CAG near the Ky Ha Peninsula, north of Chu Lai.

I arrived in Vietnam on December 26, 1966, with orders for the 3d Marine Division. Instead my orders were changed, and I was assigned to the 1st Provisional Rifle Company, which was part of MAG-36, 1st Marine Air Wing. We were all 0311s [infantry riflemen]. Our company provided perimeter and convoy security, flying medevacs, patrols, ambushes. Once in a while we even acted as door gunners for the choppers. CH-34s, the real old ones.

Our AO was the Chu Lai complex. Situated there was the big airfield, which I hardly ever saw. MAG-36 was located on the Ky Ha Peninsula; there were quite a few rivers and waterways. It was like a little delta. Outside of Ky Ha was a pretty good size village called Xam Linh, on the South China Sea. Half of our perimeter was on the South China Sea.

In early February 1967, our company gunny asked for volunteers to live in the village. About half a dozen of us went; it was boring as hell just sitting on that perimeter. Everybody was gung ho and wanted a piece of the war. The words *CAC* and *CAP* were never spoken, but that's what this was, a CAP outfit.

We had to meet one of the Marines at a break in the wire on the perimeter—real salty guy. He wasn't wearing any helmet, flak jacket, or combat boots. He was wearing sneakers! He took us in to the ville. There'd only been eight or nine Marines there before us, so now we had fifteen or sixteen. They were led by a Mexican-American sergeant who spoke fluent Vietnamese. He was sharp; you could tell he was a career Marine. Some of these guys were wearing shorts, cowboy hats, whatever they wanted, it seemed like. They didn't look like much, but they sure knew what they were doing.

Right in the middle of the ville was our CP, a masonry building of French design. I was really excited and impressed. This was what I'd been waiting for. I remember as a child reading adventure stories about the French Foreign Legion, and that's what the CAP compound in the ville reminded me of.

The Mexican sergeant explained the AO to us. This is where I learned about the Vietnamese villages. He told us that a village was not confined to just one spot; it was spread out. He said it was like a wagon wheel. The hub was the main village where the chief and elders lived, and the smaller hamlets surrounding that were like the rim of the wheel. The trails extending out from the main village to the hamlets were like the spokes, and the area between the trails was the rice paddies.

For the most part we got along fine with the villagers. We played soccer with them on our first day there. And I never had a problem with the PFs either. They were either real old or real young; there was no in-between, it seemed. They were so grateful to us for being there. I remember how happy one of them was when I put iodine on a cut he had. I equate the PFs to our minutemen in the American Revolution. They never ran, at least not in the thirty days I was there. They really loved us.

We were on the go twenty-four hours a day: ambushes, patrols, MEDCAPs, and so on. The Chu Lai AO was considered fairly secure in early 1967, even though there was quite a bit of VC activity. One of the villes near Xam Linh, in fact, was pro-VC.

In one particular hamlet there was an old man who was an informant for the CAP. Every once in a while a patrol would sneak in to get some important information from him. He had to be extremely careful because if the VC ever discovered what he was doing, he and his family would be murdered.

One night three of us went to see him—the Mexican sergeant, the radio operator, and myself. It wasn't a patrol per se, the sergeant just wanted to talk to the old man. This was the first time I had this much contact with the Vietnamese people. While the sergeant and the old man were talking, I tried to talk to his granddaughter. I showed her a picture of my '56 Oldsmobile, the first car I ever owned. I bought the thing in high school for twenty-five dollars and had to put another two hundred into it so the bomb would run! Well, she saw this picture and freaked out; she thought I was rich.

The old man gave us some hot news that night. It seemed there was a meeting of some top VC leaders nearby, in a hootch on a riverbank, not too far away. The largest VC unit in the area, I was told, was commanded by a woman who'd put a price on the heads of the CAP Marines in Xam Linh.

We made our way to this hootch and hid in the bushes and just waited. After a short time we saw shadowy figures approaching the house. Because of the curfew we knew they had to be VC. They arrived in groups of three or four. Some walked across the shallow part of the river carrying their weapons over their heads. Others came across on rafts. It took about twenty minutes until all of them were assembled; there were twenty-five or thirty of them in the hootch.

When the sergeant was satisfied no more were coming, he quietly motioned for us to move up to the hootch. We crept up to it and crouched outside, listening to the conversation inside. Of course I couldn't understand a word of Vietnamese, but the sergeant seemed to be picking up some information.

All of a sudden he turned to us and whispered, "Let's go!" Somebody was leaving the hootch and he ordered us back to the bushes. Well, I was slower than the other two guys and didn't make it back. They had made it to the bushes and were lying prone when the sergeant whispered to me, motioning at the same time, "Down! Now!" He was pissed off and said it in Spanish, but you didn't have to be a linguist to figure out what he meant. I immediately dropped and spun around in the sand. Fortunately it was a moonless night, because, except for a few small bushes, I didn't have much concealment. But I had a problem. When I fell to the ground, my M-14 got pinned under me. In the excitement I hadn't extended my arms with my weapon at the ready in case I had to use it. But it was too late: I had to stay motionless.

I saw a gook emerge from the hootch—and he was walking right toward me! My heart was racing. I thought, if this gook sees me and I have to get a round off, I'll have to get up on one knee. My only hope was the sergeant and the radio operator behind me.

As I lay there, he kept walking in my direction. I didn't think this gook thought anybody was out there; he wasn't paying attention to anything. He seemed preoccupied. Then he stopped no more than ten feet from me, did an abrupt about-face, put his weapon on the ground, dropped his drawers—and proceeded to take a shit! I swear, I thought that shit coming out of his ass was going to fall right on my face! That's how close it felt. To this day I can still smell that shit. When he finished he wiped his ass with a

Jimmy Sparrow

leaf, pulled up his pants, picked up his weapon, and strolled back to the hootch.

I was paralyzed with fear. This was the first time I had seen the enemy that close, and it was too close for me! The sergeant and radio operator crawled up to me. He chewed me out and we snuck back up to the hootch again to listen in to the meeting.

When the gathering broke up we positioned ourselves in a fork in the trail nearby. They left as they'd arrived, in groups of three and four. Then the last group left and passed by us. There was one gook lagging behind, possibly acting as a rear guard. Well, our radio operator grabbed him and beat the living hell out of him with his .45. And he made a lot of noise, too; I don't know why his buddies didn't hear it. But apparently they didn't, because no one came back to find out what happened to him. This gook was knocked out cold and bleeding like crazy from his head. Our sergeant radioed for assistance and when he felt it was safe, we ditty-bopped back to our area half-carrying, half-dragging, this unconscious gook.

The sun was coming up when we got back. We'd been out all night. First Marine Division G-2 was notified and they sent some officers in a jeep to pick this prisoner up. But before they came, our sergeant interrogated him. And he was brutal. Whenever the VC gave an unsatisfactory answer, this sergeant would club him with the butt of his M-1 carbine. I never found out what information we got. Maybe I was told, but I just don't remember. I know one thing, I'll never forget that night as long as I live.

One day ten Marines arrived at Xam Linh from the 1st Marine Division. Replacements. We were ordered back to our unit at Ky Ha, where I remained for another two months on perimeter duty. Every so often our company gunny asked the original volunteers if we wanted to go back to Xam Linh to stand watch with the PFs. I always said yes: I enjoyed being there.

In retrospect I think the Combined Action Program should have been expanded, and it would have been beneficial if more

Marines were able to speak Vietnamese. For the rest of my tour, I never had a better time with any other unit. I felt I was accomplishing something.

★ ★ ★

Since 1979 Jimmy Sparrow has been the executive director of the Connecticut-based Vietnam Veterans Agent Orange Victims, Inc. Since 1985 the VVAOVI, through the Brandie Schieb Children's Fund, has provided nationwide assistance to more than a hundred children of Vietnam veterans with medical bills due to birth defects and chronic health problems.

In addition to serving as treasurer for the Greater Stamford Veterans Council, Sparrow is a former commander of VFW Post 10013 and American Legion Post 3 in Stamford, Connecticut, and VFW Post 6933 in Darien, Connecticut.

Lt. Col. William R. Corson, USMC (Ret.)

Director, Combined Action Program
1967–1968

A driving force behind the Combined Action Program, Lieutenant Colonel Corson became its first director in February 1967. Through his tireless efforts, the CAPs finally were organized and developed their own table of organization. Opinionated and outspoken, Corson vehemently opposed Westmoreland's strategy in Vietnam. Retiring from the Marine Corps in 1968, he wrote his first book, The Betrayal *(1968), criticizing the allied pacification efforts during the Vietnam War.*

Although the Marine Corps had an experience in Latin America some years back, in what was called at that time guerrilla wars, it is not accurate to establish that experience as an analogy to the Combined Action Program in Vietnam. There are some similarities, but the war itself, the enemy, and the political situation were very different from the Latin American counterparts. There the United States was involved in a form of Yankee imperialism that had little to do with the reasons we entered Vietnam.

The Combined Action Program got started in Vietnam in ad hoc form: there was a necessity to provide air-base security for the aircraft flying in and around the Chu Lai and Phu Bai areas. This attempt to neutralize the potential effect of civilians directly adjacent to an AO led to the use of locals to aid, not so much in the security of the airfields, but in preventing a surprise assault on the facilities.

Later on, Gen. Wallace M. Greene, Jr., then Commandant of the Marine Corps, along with Lt. Gen. Victor "Brute" Krulak and Lt. Gen. Lewis W. Walt, Commanding General, III MAF, decided to adopt the CAPs. What we were concerned with was not only protecting the airfields, because the Marine regiments had already moved beyond the protection of airfields into the countryside, but also protecting our lines of communication. That means your supplies and personnel, too. So it became necessary that the enemy be denied access to the hamlets along these important lines of communication. And as our TAORs expanded, so did the number of CAP hamlet requirements.

When I took command of the program, we did not have a TO/E. We could not program requests for manpower, material, and so forth, against an authorized organization; we were detailing Marines from line units to serve in the program. Part of it was negotiating with some of my friends and peers who realized that by giving up some of their troops, they were enhancing their own security in their TAORs.

The men I wanted to come into the Combined Action Program had to have line experience. They had to know what it meant to take another human being's life, and how to shoot, move, and communicate.

This is not to say I was looking for the kill-crazy types or psychotics. Sadly, you occasionally run into people like that. On the other hand, I wasn't looking for bleeding heart liberals, either.

I was looking for well-trained Marines. Marines that had not gone so far into the bamboo that they were unable to empathize with the Vietnamese people. If they entered the job with an ethnocentric attitude, they would not succeed. They had to think on their own, be proud, loyal, and brave. And they had to have open minds to a new experience. That is why, I felt, the combat experience was very important. Until you have been involved in the business of killing, you can't appreciate the tragedy of warfare.

I also realized that it was not possible to transform these Marines into linguists or cultural anthropologists overnight. However, it was possible to teach them some of the customs, some of the history, some of the culture of Vietnam. Maybe then they would approach the Vietnamese in the hamlets as human beings. Not as dinks, slopes, and gooks, but as people with families not unlike their own.

Fortunately, the majority of men I was able to recruit did measure up. If they didn't, all the CAP leader had to do was say that a certain individual didn't have it and that individual was gone. This is not to say that the Marine couldn't do well in another unit.

Also, there is a danger that someone who has experienced quite a bit of death and destruction will communicate despair to those around him, whereas we had to convey a sense of hope that we would prevail—not necessarily succeed, but at least prevail.

I remember being teased because I showed the CAP Marines

how to eat a meal in a Vietnamese home, how to play elephant chess, how to be accepted in a Vietnamese environment and perform a very difficult mission. They never let me down—not once.

One of the great difficulties in Vietnam, after the Geneva Accords of 1954, was that many of the people had come down from the north and could not identify with the southerners. A number of them went to work for the Diem government in various capacities, but they weren't the kids on the block. That was a very serious problem.

And then there was nationalism; Ho Chi Minh used it to his advantage. Vietnamese nationalism involved a commitment and an ideology bigger than we ever dreamed of.

In *The Betrayal* [1968] I wrote about the relocation of people from one village to another. The Vietnamese, who had lived in these hamlets for hundreds of years, had probably never traveled more than fifty or sixty miles from the place of their birth—ever. And here the U.S. government uproots them and moves them as part of this Strategic Hamlet Program, not realizing the tremendous shock this was causing.

The PFs were probably the most misunderstood element of manpower available to the Republic of South Vietnam [RSVN]. They were abused at times, but they were the building blocks upon which a successful strategy in Vietnam could have been based. No matter what country a person lives in, that person will defend his family and home.

Most CAP Marines learned not to look down their noses at the PFs because their very lives could depend upon them. They had to shape them up. This was hard at the onset, but it did develop. The people of Vietnam who were protected by the CAPs thought highly of the Marines. We didn't have the attitude of the French or the Chinese who had previously occupied the country.

The NVA is one of the finest groups of light infantry you'll find anywhere, but as far as a people, there was no difference between them and the PFs. They were both Vietnamese. I believe that the Asian soldier—Japanese, Chinese, Vietnamese—is as good as anybody walking down the street. However, his capacity as a fighting man is dependent upon training and leadership. When Asian troops are properly led, they fight extremely well.

But this CAP program did not come together overnight. In 1966, President Lyndon B. Johnson made a trip to Southeast Asia, where a big conference was held in the Philippines and attended by all the top commanders in Vietnam. This was right after the success of the Marines in Operation Hastings, where serious damage was inflicted upon several NVA battalions that tried to invade South Vietnam across the DMZ. It was one of the few conventional battles fought in the war, and it prompted then-Senator George Aiken of Vermont to suggest declaring a victory and getting out. And it was a victory we could have gotten out on, by the way.

The meeting in the Philippines was prophetic. LBJ was happy he had a success, and it looked like we were going to be the big winners. LBJ wanted to get rid of all the communists in South Vietnam.

Lt. Gen. Lew Walt, Commander of I Corps, was at the meeting and he came back spreading the word. I was invited to attend a meeting in Da Nang at III MAF Headquarters because, in addition to my own battalion, I was also in charge of the Southern Sector Command, which included 4,000 Marines and sailors.

After General Walt told us what was decided in the Philippines, the other division and regimental commanders requested additional equipment and supplies. Then General Walt asked if there were any questions. I knew Lew Walt quite well so I raised my hand and said, "General, I have one question. Whose fuckin' dumb idea was this?"

We had moved from a strategy that entailed targets of opportunity, which Hastings was, to a strategy of attrition. Call it search and destroy, it's still attrition. We were forgetting our history. The strategy of attrition, coupled with search and destroy, was a loser. It doesn't work.

You can win a war with a flawed strategy and suitable tactics, or with flawed tactics and a suitable strategy. But you cannot win a war when your strategy and your tactics are both flawed.

After I returned from that meeting, I called my S-3 officer and we sat under a tree that night and talked. These people, I told him, meaning Johnson and the others, have lost their minds. Henceforth, our mission must be to save as many Marine lives as possible. And this meant to keep our Vietnamese allies alive in the hamlets as well. We could engage the enemy, but to chase him all over the bloomin' barnyard was pure nonsense.

By summer 1965 we'd eliminated a counter-intelligence effort that had been in place, designed to ascertain who in the ARVN and the South Vietnamese government was working for the other side. In other words, who the communists were. And this was a conscious decision.

When Saigon fell in April 1975, there was an NVA general on the platform who had been an ARVN colonel working in the combined chiefs of staff office. Our TAORs in many cases had been adjacent to ARVN units. To protect shooting up the ARVN, you had to let them know when you were going to be operating in their area, so we had warning orders issued. There was one operation called Starlite in August 1965 in which we didn't let the ARVN know, and we had tactical surprise. But after that we had to inform them. And the guy we were sending that information to was a communist! Warning orders issued to U.S. forces were in the hands of the communists before they even reached our guys. So the NVA could decline combat when they wanted to and fight when it was to their advantage.

So the 1965 suspension of the CIA's capability to carry out counter-intelligence penetration of the RSVN and their military, along with the 1966 meeting that embodied the strategy of attrition, enabled us to go from victory that would have been difficult but feasible to defeat that was inevitable. But in getting to that defeat, there was quite a bit of tragedy.

The CAPs were not able by themselves, because they were out there as a slender reed, to do it all. They did keep some Vietnamese alive and protect them from the horrors of war. Since CAP locations were on the lines of communication, this facilitated the security of the Marine installations as well as operations from these installations. And CAP Marines did kill their quota of the enemy, but the strategy of search and destroy did not benefit the CAPs.

Gen. William Westmoreland, head of the U.S. Military Assistance Command, Vietnam [MACV], did not approve of the CAPs. In his book *A Soldier Reports* [1976] he damned them with faint praise, saying in effect that yes, it was an interesting experiment, but it was obvious that it could not be applied throughout the country.

Robert McNamara, then-Secretary of Defense, was never given the opportunity to approve or disapprove of the CAPs because we could not move it through the jungle of the Joint Chiefs of Staff. And that is not just a glib overstatement.

Some of our allies, especially the ones I knew, thought the CAP program was the wisest thing in Vietnam. But they also were attuned to the political realities and realized that General Westmoreland and the Army did not believe that this was the way to fight this particular war. Not necessarily this kind of war but this particular war, the war in Vietnam.

The Marine Corps in Vietnam had to fight in accordance with the war of attrition, but that strategy was developed exclusive of what the Marine Corps felt about the Combined Action Program.

Let me read from an unclassified top-secret message that General Westmoreland sent to Gen. Earle Wheeler, Chairman of the Joint Chiefs of Staff, on January 22, 1968 [National Archives, 830024]. The importance of this message is, of course, that the Tet Offensive came shortly thereafter. Also, this communication was sent back channel and the Marine Corps did not have the opportunity to comment on it or refute it. This was certainly not the official Army position, but it represented what General Westmoreland thought of the Marine Corps.

> Subject: Visit to Washington by Richard E. Cabazos, LTC INF, USA.
>
> 1. The above-named officer will arrive in Washington on 25 January on a TDY status per my orders for several days. This officer has just finished ten months in command of the 1st Battalion, 18th Infantry, of the 1st Infantry Division, and in my opinion is one of the top battalion commanders in Vietnam. He is a disciplinarian, tactician, and a commander whose results have been nothing short of spectacular. During the 4th quarter of CY 1967, his battalion killed 875 of the enemy with only 19 soldiers killed within the battalion. Because of his competence, I have recently sent him to the dye marker area (DMZ) to spend ten days with the Marines to advise them on how to construct a battalion defensive position. The Marines were very receptive to his advice and reportedly respected his professionalism.
>
> 2. I urge that you receive Cabazos and plan on talking to him for at least an hour. The reason that I make this suggestion is because of his insight into Marine philosophy, doctrine, and leadership. As you perhaps appreciate, the military professionalism of the Marines falls far short of the standards that should be demanded by our Armed Forces. Indeed, they are brave and proud, but their standards, tactics, and lack of command supervision throughout their ranks require improvement in the national interest.
>
> 3. Needless to say, reorientation of this situation would be quite a task, and it cannot be done overnight. However, as I

review the matter in broad perspective, you are the only individual that will understand and could possibly initiate some action to bring about a change. Perhaps this is a matter you do not choose to touch, and this I would understand. However, I am frustrated by the problem, am concerned as a military man, and feel it my duty to give you the benefit of my views.

4. Having said all this, there are many things that commend the Marines, but I would be less than frank if I did not say that I feel somewhat insecure with the situation in Quang Tri Province, in view of my knowledge of their shortcomings. Without question, many lives would be saved if their tactical professionalism were enhanced.

5. If you do not choose to see Cabazos, I will stop him. Otherwise, he will be on his way to see you today. Best regards.

I don't think it's necessary for Bill Corson to editorialize General Westmoreland's innermost thoughts, but in my opinion this is one of the major reasons we lost the war in Vietnam. The Westmorelands of the U.S. Army did not know how to fight it, and they wouldn't let us fight it in a way in which victory could have been achieved.

So how much support did they give the Combined Action Program? They gave it shit! And the reason they gave it shit was that their own shortcomings would be revealed. The tragic end in Vietnam demonstrated this.

What were some of the good experiences from the Combined Action Program? Well, in the morning when we would brief General Walt and the other members of the III MAF staff, there were times when I would say, "The CAPs had a good night last night—470,000 Vietnamese people got a good night's sleep and no Marines got killed in the provision of that good night's sleep."

The bad times were the same as those in every other war I'd been in. When I had to look at the faces and the maimed bodies of my fallen comrades. They were Marines, but they were my kids, too. They died trying to aid the people of South Vietnam to remain free. And there's nothing wrong with that. The things that brought us to Vietnam were not wrong. When it becomes wrong is when you don't know how to do it. But we knew how to do it.

I recall several hamlets that took a real heavy hit. The Vietnamese people showed a genuine sense of tragedy and grief, not only for their citizens and PFs, but for those young Marines who had died defending them and their homes. And this grief cannot be faked! The notion that life is cheap in the Orient is a bunch of bullshit!

The CAPs were a success, and it was reported by people like Ward Just and William Lederer in *Life* magazine and several newspapers. But good news doesn't make it in the newspapers. The good news of 114 hamlets where 470,000 Vietnamese people were able to go about their business isn't exciting enough. They wanted children being napalmed on the highway.

But we could have done better. I told this to Ward Just: Give me 15,000 Marines and move the rest of these people around here in a more sensible way and the communists will not own enough territory to carry on their activities. It would have taken two more years. I said that in 1967. There was no doubt in my mind about it.

The Marines in the Combined Action Program accepted their responsibilities and tried to do a good job. Good God, some of them had three Purple Hearts and they still wanted to stay with the Vietnamese people! They understood what it was all about— as a people, as a nation, as Marines. They can look at themselves in the mirror today and realize that. And the people of Vietnam know it, too. I know this from some CAP veterans who have returned to Vietnam.

Here's a good case in point: Two CAPs with PFs guarding the egress from Da Nang during the 1968 Tet Offensive were wiped out to the last man. However, they held until elements of the 1st Marine Division could arrive and eventually destroy two NVA divisions who were trying to seize the city. Those CAP Marines and PFs knew they couldn't make it out in time. Twenty-five men died; one was severely wounded and is still in a Veteran's Administration hospital today.

The young men who demonstrated this extraordinary heroism were given appropriate awards some years later. On a per capita basis, CAP Marines won 240 percent more Navy Crosses than Marines in other units. Why is that important? For an enlisted man to receive a Navy Cross—and live—is equivalent to a Medal of Honor in some of the other services. Remarkable.

There was a young corporal at that egress near Da Nang who had a 60-mm mortar we had scrounged. He said to me, "Don't worry about it Colonel—we'll hold 'em!"

They did.

★　　★　　★

Lt. Col. William R. Corson's career included special and secret intelligence operations with the British, Japanese, and Korean intelligence services and each of the U.S. intelligence agencies and departments; service as a naval attaché; membership on the U.S. Country Team for Communist China and Far East Inter-Agency Defector Committee; Staff Secretary of the President's Special Group (CI) joint DOD-CIA Committee on Counterinsurgency; Special Assistant to the Secretary of Defenses's Director of the Advanced Research Projects Agency; and Officer in Charge of the Assistant Secretary of Defense (Systems Analysis) Southeast Asia intelligence evaluation program.

Since his retirement, Lieutenant Colonel Corson has served as an aide and confidant to former White House staffers and as an unofficial adviser to various members of the national security and intelligence community and congressional committees. He has also served as an adjunct professor of economics at Howard University and as a vice president of operations at Research Incorporated. Since 1972 he has written the monthly "Vietnam Veterans Adviser" column that appears in Penthouse *magazine. He is also the author of several books.*

Lt. Col.
William R.
Corson

1968

Tet

"We have reached an important point when the end begins to come into view," said an optimistic General William Westmoreland on November 21, 1967, at the National Press Club in Washington, D.C. While Westmoreland was delivering these glowing reports in the United States, the communists were preparing to launch the 1968 Tet Offensive. On January 30, 1968, enemy attacks erupted throughout South Vietnam. Thirty-six provincial capitals, five cities, numerous district capitals and hamlets, and twenty-three airfields and bases were assaulted.

One of the CAPs' primary missions was to collect intelligence. Had they failed to see the approaching Tet Offensive?

Such does not seem to be the case. In fact, according to former director Colonel Byron F. Brady, "it was the CAPs that gave the first and decisive intelligence by which III MAF canceled the Tet cease-fire agreement with the National Liberation Front prior to the actual breakout of hostilities" (Peterson 1989, 56).

Before the offensive, many CAPs were reporting increased enemy activity in their AOs. B. Keith Cossey in CAP Echo-4 said, "For a week or more our village [Lo Giang] had suddenly been filled with strange young men in civilian clothes."

Jack Lofland from Alpha-2 said, "Early in December 1967 some of the villagers started asking me to give them sandbags. . . . I changed the [patrol] routine by going into some of the houses. . . . the villagers were actually digging in" (Hammel 1991).

On January 12, 1968, a daytime patrol conducted by the Marines and PFs from Alpha-2 was ambushed. Pinned down, the patrol was finally saved by F-4B Phantoms from the Da Nang Air Base. Lofland discovered later that elements of a newly arrived NVA regiment had ambushed his patrol.

In November 1967, a patrol from CAP Hotel-6 had uncovered a relief map, prepared in the ground, depicting all the CAP units south of Phu Bai to the Hai Van Pass. The information was passed to the CACO commander and forwarded to the G-2 section of the 3d Marine Division. No action was taken.

If the CAPs had been reporting these findings to the proper authorities, why was nothing done?

Tom Krusewski, a member of Hotel-6, was frustrated. "That was one of the problems with the CAPs—we didn't have any officers with us. They thought we exaggerated."

Another CAP Marine, 1st Sergeant Gene Beck, was angry. "We were not listened to by higher command . . . we watched them move in with rockets. One-twenty-twos and 140-mm rockets, and heavy mortars. We were told by the higher-ups that, quote, we didn't know what the hell we were talking about" (Peterson 1989, 56).

The CAPs were hit hard during the 1968 Tet Offensive. It seemed as if the enemy was aware of the value of the CAPs and made a concerted effort to eliminate as many as possible. From December 1967 to January 1968 the CAPs averaged five contacts with the enemy per week. From January 29 to February 9 there were fifteen contacts per week.

Tragically, it appears that the intelligence collected by various CAPs warning of the impending 1968 Tet Offensive was not taken seriously.

Harvey Baker

3d CAG
1967–1968

During the Hill Fights in the spring of 1967, Harvey Baker's unit, Company K, 3d Battalion, 3d Marines, sustained horrendous casualties. Surviving the ordeal, he sought transfer to a CAP unit and was sent to Alpha-2, south of Hue City.

When I first got to Vietnam I thought, Damn, this isn't going to be bad. I landed in Da Nang and saw all the tents and said, Shit, this is gonna be alright.

I went up north to Dong Ha after I was processed and was assigned to Kilo Company, 3d Battalion, 3d Marines. They were loading body bags onto a chopper. These were the first dead bodies I had seen since I got there.

My MOS was 0331—machine gunner—I was in weapons platoon. But when I got there, I walked point out of Ca Lu. New guys were usually picked to walk point; it was the most dangerous job. I got good at it, though. I could sense and see different things before they happened.

I fought at Hill 861. Our company went up that hill—eighteen of us walked off. We'd just got the M-16s, and half of 'em jammed up. The cartridges swelled up in the chamber. I said, If there's a God, why is he allowing this to happen to these young people? Then I said to hell with God. This is just suriving. And I'm still in that survival mode.

We went back to the rear to reform our company when I heard they had some CAP openings. I'd heard about these CAP units and thought this was my chance to get out of the bush. They accepted me and a guy named Nesbitt.

We went to Phu Bai and went through a little training, things like Vietnamese culture, radio procedure, that type of stuff. Nice and clean. That's where I started smoking pot and learning about Black Power. I was pretty tight with the dope pushers. You could get anything you wanted—beer, whiskey, dope. I never messed

Harvey Baker

with no whiskey, just pot. Smoked it all the time. I'd become kill crazy. And if I wasn't killin', I had to be high. Smokin' pot was a way to make me forget about what was happenin'.

My CAP was Alpha-2, south of Hue. Daytime there was nice, but nighttime could be hell. I was in a double CAP: we had two squads of nine men. We never wore flak jackets, helmets, or anything like that. One squad would go out on a night ambush damn near every night, and the other would stand bunker watch or be a reactionary force in case the ambush squad got into trouble.

When we made contact and got some kills, we'd bring back the bodies and lay them near the ville in this pagoda. If the dead were related to anybody in the ville, they'd come and claim them. Most villagers wouldn't get the dead bodies because they were afraid we'd retaliate against them. Sometimes the bodies would just lay there for a long time and rot.

The PFs went out on patrol with us. Usually there were six Marines and eight PFs, maybe more, depending on the intelligence reports that told us about the enemy in our AO. The PFs would hang canteens and things off their cartridge belts that would make noise and alert the enemy. As far as the PFs go, I didn't trust most of 'em. There were some good ones that would stay and fight with you, but others would just run off. When our ville was overrun during Tet of '67, three PFs were found dead. There were supposed to be thirty-two in the ville. Where were the rest?

Our ville was near the Ashau Valley. There was this mountain behind the ville where the NVA or VC would come through to get food and stuff from the villagers. When we went on patrol, four or five of us would drop back and set up an ambush. We called these killer teams. One night eight of us set up an ambush. I was with two guys from New York, one named Joe. He was kill crazy. The other was Norman. Norman didn't give a shit. He was with the 1st Battalion, 9th Marines before he came to CAP. Anyway, we caught 'em walking through and hit 'em hard. We must've killed a hundred of 'em that night.

Then we got this sergeant from Tennessee. Evidently he was

going to be busted, so they sent him to CAP. He didn't like blacks. Up until then, everybody got along. He would say the Vietnamese word for black to the PFs, but he meant nigger.

One night this sergeant came out on a killer team with me. We got in an argument and he called me a nigger. I told him what I thought about that. And then he shot at me. I stabbed him, and I was definitely trying to kill him.

They sent me to Phu Bai under arrest. The next day the fighting at Hue City broke out and I was heli-lifted back to help Alpha-6 CAP, which was in danger of being overrun. The gooks threw satchel charges into the bunkers. I was in a hole with this one guy who was firing an M-60 machine gun. He was shooting at this dude all night long. He told me he had killed him once. What the VC had done was tie this dead gook to a tombstone and this guy I was with kept firing at him. They had to medevac him out; he'd lost it.

As far as the grunt officers go, it's like everything else, there were good ones and bad ones. I saw officers go on patrol with us and others would just sit back on their asses and let you walk into some shit.

Every unit I was in was good. My CAP was good until that sergeant got there and busted it all up. We were all together before that. I was promoted to sergeant in the weapons platoon before I was busted.

I think our CAP made some of those Vietnamese in the ville rich. They washed our clothes and we bought food from them. They made some money.

As far as our relationship with the Vietnamese people, the CAP did give us a chance to really get to know them. They were just ordinary people raising families and things, instead of being just another gook.

I was fighting for the civil rights of the Vietnamese, so they could live free. But my civil rights as a black American back in the United States were fucked up. And it's still fucked up.

Damn! I think about all the blood that was shed. And it doesn't make a difference what color you were. What a shame! I really didn't see any hope for the whole thing.

*   *   *

Harvey Baker is currently enrolled in a drug-rehabilitation program in Wichita, Kansas, for assault and substance-abuse charges. He is married with three daughters.

John Balanco

3d CAG
1967–1968

John Balanco did two tours of duty in Vietnam, one in 1965–66 with the 3d Tank Battalion and the other as a CAP Marine. The Oscar CAP he was assigned to was one of the few that worked with Montagnards. He is a survivor of the seventy-seven-day siege of Khe Sanh and was awarded a Silver Star for his actions at the battle of Khe Sanh Village.

In trying to recall my experiences of twenty-five years ago, I have rediscovered feelings and emotions that I had buried in a mental time capsule. Keeping all that entombed in my soul as deep as possible has been an everyday job since 1968. I am very proud of my service as a Marine, mostly being a CAP Marine. But having killed, having seen hundreds of people blown apart leaves me with no sense of glory.

The whole experience was like a painting on glass that broke. Each of us walked away with a few pieces of the glass, and it has only been in the past year that I have wanted to reconstruct the whole painting. I hope future combat vets will learn from our experiences so they can deal with the true horrors of war.

I reported to the Huong Hoa District Headquarters on January 19, 1968, and I was assigned the position of senior adviser and Marine squad leader of CAP Oscar-1 at the peaceful, beautiful village of Khe Sanh. There was also a four-man U.S. Army Advisory Team.

Khe Sanh is in the northwestern corner of South Vietnam, next to Laos and North Vietnam, high up in the mountains. There was a heavenly feeling about it and I was happy to be there. The local Montagnard tribesmen, called Bru, were a very different and wonderful people. It was all like nothing I'd ever seen before.

Early in the morning of January 21, visibility conditions were bad due to a heavy fog. I was checking with the men on watch when suddenly we were assaulted by the 66th NVA Regiment, about 2,500 strong, with mortars, rockets, and artillery.

Our forces numbered about 175—14 CAP Oscar-1 Marines; our CO, Lieutenant Stamper; our gunny, Staff Sergeant Boyda; two Vietnamese platoons from the 915th RF Company; U.S. Army Advisory personnel Capt. Bruce Clarke, Medic Sfc. James Perry, Sergeant King, and Sergeant Kasper; and the rest were Bru.

The camp was arranged in a set of compartmented squares with a triangular French fort attached. The 915th RF Company was on the south end, Oscar-1 on the north. In the middle of the triangle, Lieutenant Stamper and Captain Clarke shared the CP with the South Vietnamese commander, Lieutenant Nhi, and his staff. The other Army personnel occupied a bunker in the front of the compound. Out in the village were four Vietnamese nurses: Coh Dang, Coh Chanh, Coh Ninh, and Coh Lieu. They would soon be burdened beyond anyone's imagination.

The battle for Khe Sanh village lasted thirty-six hours. The NVA surrounded us and then started a massive ground attack in human waves. Most of the heaviest fighting was in the early morning, when the fog was the thickest. But even with their overwhelming numbers, they did not overrun our compound. Not one NVA soldier made it into our camp.

Cpl. Verner R. Russell countered the assault on the northeast corner with his machine gun and his Bru A-gunner. These two were incredible. Some of the enemy made it to within thirty feet of the wire, but not beyond. NVA bodies were stacked like match sticks all around Russell's sector. He was awarded the Silver Star for that battle. Tremendous credit also goes to Cpl. Lou Loshelder, Cpl. S. J. Dilley, Lance Corporal Dahler, L. Cpl. Ulysses Reyes, L. Cpl. Jose Ramos, L. Cpl. Antonio Vera, Lance Corporal Whiting, and Lance Corporal Breedlove. They courageously defended the north and west sides of the camp, near the main entrance.

The two exhausted platoons from the RF company were under constant attack on the southwest side. Around 0900 I placed three Marines with them: L. Cpl. Howard McKinnis, L. Cpl. Frank Batchman, and L. Cpl. C. E. "Butch" Still. I knew this would give the 915th a boost in morale; those three Marines were very inspirational and brave. I wanted to write them up for medals but was never given the opportunity.

During the initial fighting I was wounded by shrapnel in the left foot and hand. To the best of my knowledge, I was the only person except Medic Perry who was roving the entire compound. Captain Clarke and Lieutenant Stamper manned the radios to the combat base that supplied the artillery for our defense. More than 1,000 variable time shells burst around our compound. We also received spectacular precision bombing from Marine and Air Force jets. The artillery and air strikes seemed to startle and immobilize the NVA, and I think that was the main reason we weren't overrun. Besides this, Captain Clarke was on the radio with Bob Brewer, the Quang Tri Province senior adviser, trying to coordinate a relief force. He was also on a third radio with Captain Britt, an Air Force forward air controller [FAC], who was flying above us. They teamed up for twenty of the best air strikes you can imagine.

As I came upon the southwest side, I noticed a machine gun that wasn't firing, in a tall bunker built out of sandbags, eight or nine feet high. It was a critical machine gun that had jammed, and the RFs had abandoned the position. I went up and pulled the pin on the tripod to carry it down, but an NVA soldier fired an RPG at me. The explosion lifted me and the machine gun and slammed us back four or five feet, and the right side of my head went numb. I suffered a concussion that still troubles me today.

I jumped up and screamed to a Marine to give me his M-79 grenade launcher. Then I scored a direct hit on the group of NVA about forty feet away. I could actually see body parts flying all over the place. Right after that the men of the 915th started firing furiously at the oncoming NVA.

Around 1130 the fog burned off, and in the next five hours there were three attempts to resupply and reinforce us. The first was when the Vietnamese and Bru were running low on M-1 and carbine ammo. Helicopters couldn't land, so they hovered over the front of our compound and kicked it out.

On the second try, Lieutenant Chapman led Delta Company, 1/26, from the combat base to try to reach us at the ville. They were the only reaction company in reserve. Captain Clarke was in constant communication with Lieutenant Chapman. Delta Company reached the top of Hill 471 at the edge of the ville and could see Vietnamese, but before they could relieve us, Lt. Col. James Wilkerson, the battalion commander, changed his mind and ordered them back. He probably thought it was too dangerous and they would be ambushed.

Late in the afternoon of January 21, the third and final reactionary force tried to reach us. They were the 256th RF Company, led by Lt. Col. Joseph Seymoe. That attempt was catastrophic.

They tried to land at the old French fort on the outskirts of the ville, but the NVA mauled them badly. In terms of proportionate casualties and equipment losses, this air assault would be the worst military debacle of the entire Khe Sanh campaign. Thirteen American pilots, fourteen other crew members, and seventy-four RF soldiers were dead or missing after it was over; Seymoe's body was recovered from the site months later by the 1st Air Cav.

On the morning of January 22, Stamper and Boyda told me to put together a patrol and head out in an attempt to link up with any survivors. I took four Marines and eight Bru with me, all volunteers. This mixed group patrolled down the road toward the old French fort, which sat on a hill just to the right of Route 9. We were skittish and also awed at all the death and destruction.

We made it to the bottom of the hill and saw three or four uniformed soldiers up on a bunker. I thought they were the Vietnamese from the 256th RFs. Corporal Russell asked if I was sure they were from the 256th, because they were off in the distance and we couldn't really see their uniforms clearly. We waved and yelled at them to come on down, and they waved back for us to come on up. They never spoke a word, so I got suspicious and took the patrol back to the camp. They had to be NVA setting us up for an ambush.

When we got back to the compound, a few of us searched through the dead NVA. We were outside the wire for only a few minutes, but I saw at least a hundred dead bodies just on the west side of the compound. We gathered rifles, RPG weapons, and personal effects from the bodies. Many of the AK-47s and AK-44s were brand new; some still had Cosmoline on them. We recovered the first RPG-7s ever seen in Vietnam and more than 150 weapons. Lieutenant Stamper later told me that the FAC estimated as many as 800 NVA killed or wounded in the area surrounding the ville.

That night we received only sniper fire and a few mortar rounds. In the early morning hours of January 22, CAP Oscar-2 Marines made it into our wire. They had been attacked at the same time we were. They were Sgt. Roy Harper, Cpl. Dan Sullivan, Cpl. John Tullis, Corporal Harper, L. Cpl. Nick Cruz, Lance Corporal Tyson, Private First Class Biddle, and Pfc Daniel Matonias. Navy Corpsman John Roberts and some Bru were also in the group.

That same morning, a helicopter picked up Lieutenant Stamper and flew him back to the combat base. We didn't know that the base had taken a lot of incoming and the ammo dump had ex-

John Balanco holds his cut-off M-1 carbine. The weapons on the cloth were taken from the NVA at Khe Sanh.

ploded. Most of the hills manned by Marines were under attack as well. Over 40,000 NVA had surrounded us and we were going to consolidate our forces—about 5,000.

We received a radio message some hours later from Lieutenant Stamper telling us to pack up: 8,000 to 9,000 NVA were headed our way. Since the ammo dump had been hit, the base could no longer support us, so we were ordered to abandon the ville. The wounded were evacuated first, and no RFs or Bru with their weapons were allowed on the helicopters. We did not agree with this order; it made us all very angry. We'd fought alongside the Bru and they were extremely loyal. But, being Marines, we followed orders. Even those we disagreed with.

As we were pulling out, a group of frightened Vietnamese civilians rushed toward the chopper from the north side of the LZ. So many of them were hanging onto the chopper that it couldn't take off, and we had to physically push them off it. I fired a few M-79 rounds into a tree line on the south side, and the sounds made the Vietnamese stay back. There were six evacuation missions that day.

Hundreds of dead bodies were around and scores of people

were asking to be evacuated. Two civilians carrying a Bru on a stretcher approached me. He had been burnt by napalm, and they asked me to let him on the last chopper out. His body was blown up like a balloon. I had never seen anything like that before; I was sure he was dead. But the pilot said in no uncertain terms that no one except Americans could go on the last chopper out and he was departing right now.

Captain Clarke and his Army advisers finally got orders from Bob Brewer to withdraw. Clarke decided that they would walk with the Bru and RFs to the compound at the combat base, and he radioed ahead. They made it. I've always admired them. They all received Bronze Stars.

I was the last Marine to get out on the last helicopter leaving Khe Sanh village. As we lifted off, the ville looked like there had been a massacre. What a horrible sight!

A Special Forces strike team conducted a raid that afternoon to destroy the equipment that had been left behind. They were led by Major Simcox and Captain Clarke. Then came the air strikes and artillery and the huge B-52 raids that continued for two and a half months.

Ray Stubbe, chaplain for 1/26, estimates that 5,000 Bru were killed during the battle for Khe Sanh. Over 1,000 Bru were evacuated to a resettlement camp at Cam Lo, and about 3,000 tried to walk down Route 9 to reach Cam Lo. Only 1,643 made it. Others found safe havens in Laos. The Bru never complained that they had been betrayed.

We never talked about it. All of us felt sad and hurt that the decision was made by the higher command to abandon the Bru. These were the people we were fighting with and fighting for. Now we were abandoning them? It still makes me feel outraged and hopeless.

When we reached Khe Sanh combat base we joined up with Lieutenant Stamper, who told us we were not going to stay on the Marine base. We were to stay at FOB-3 [forward operating base], manned by Green Berets and their indigenous forces. Captain Clarke joined up with us, and our Bru helped us defend the south end of FOB-3. There were fifty Green Berets and twenty-seven Marines at FOB-3. CAP Oscar-3 linked up with us also: Sgt. Tom Corcoran, Craig A. Rowe, John Reifsnider, Freeman Taylor, Garcia, Meadows, Jones, Walker, and Harding.

Our area was just an open trench line with a few strands of barbed wire. I still have photographs of what FOB-3 looked like when we first arrived, and seventy-seven days later when the siege was over. By March '68 we had built reinforced bunkers with roofs three feet thick. It's amazing what a few thousand rounds of incoming will do to inspire people to great achievements. I found out later that more bombs were dropped in a five-mile radius around Khe Sanh during the siege than in all of the Pacific in World War II.

There's not much written about FOB-3. The SOG [Studies and Observations Group] personnel ran secret missions into Laos and North Vietnam from there. Black helicopters with no markings landed and took men dressed in civilian clothes away. None of them ever returned. This went on throughout the siege.

Some days, the NVA threw over 1,000 rounds of incoming at us, trying to knock out the million-dollar bunker. There were rumors that's what it cost to build. SOG had electronic equipment inside the bunker that could pick up sounds from sensors that had been dropped all over the border area. They even picked up Russian. They learned from their Laotian sources that the NVA had tanks, but no one believed them until several weeks later. That's when the NVA overran the Special Forces camp at Lang Vei, using tanks.

We started running patrols with the Green Berets. There was a reward of thirty days' R and R to anywhere in the world for those who captured an NVA officer. We'd go out at night in groups of three or four, and the Green Berets wanted to go with us because most of the CAP Marines and the Bru knew the terrain well. We accompanied them on a few patrols until one of them was accidentally killed with his own claymore. From then on we ran our own stuff; just Marines and Bru.

We felt segregated and isolated at FOB-3. The Green Berets had steak, beer, and hard liquor, but we were not even allowed on the combat base with our Bru. Col. David Lownds, 26th Marines regimental commander, didn't want any armed Bru on the camp; I guess he didn't trust them. A company from the 37th ARVN Ranger Company was dug in outside the wire as well, near the airstrip.

A short distance from us were several Marine tanks with their turrets turned and their guns pointed directly at us, and Cambodian mercenaries were entrenched right behind us. They were being paid by SOG personnel to guard the million-dollar bunker. I went back to speak with them, communicating with their leader as best as I could in sign language and broken English. Neither of us knew what we would be experiencing in the coming days, and I thought it would be to our mutual advantage to work together. I asked him if we got hit could we use their trench as a second line of defense. Their leader, a man old enough to be my father, made it perfectly clear that he was fighting for money. If we attempted to fall back to their position, they would kill us.

Marine tanks and Cambodian mercenaries behind us and NVA in front—we were definitely on our own. I now knew what it felt like to be abandoned, like the Bru.

I recall one day in particular: February 26. We were watching jets drop their ordnance right outside our wire. I was talking to L. Cpl. Billy Livingston, and after I finished I got up and sat down not twenty feet away from him. Suddenly one of the jets mistakenly let go his bombs inside our compound and a large piece of shrapnel took Livingtston's head right off. I walked over, took his wallet and dog tags, and gave them to Staff Sergeant Boyda. Corpsman John Roberts and a few others put him in a body bag. Then I sat down and finished a can of beans and franks before gathering our group to say a prayer for Livingston. By this time most of us were numb to our feelings, which helped us to survive Khe Sanh, I'm sure. I have often wondered, during the past year, if you can train for such numbness. I have concluded that it's impossible; it just comes with combat experience.

★   ★   ★

John Balanco lives in San Ramon, California, with his wife and son. He is a General Engineering contractor. He serves on the board of directors and is chairperson of the fund-raising committee for the Khe Sanh Veterans, Inc., which is committed to humanitarian projects for the Bru. In April 1993 he returned to Khe Sanh to participate in a television documentary and spend time with the Bru survivors of the battle for Khe Sanh.

Tom Harvey

2d and 3d CAGs
January–July 1968; May 1969–March 1970

In his first tour with the program, Tom Harvey was assigned to CAP Delta-1 near Da Nang. When he returned in 1969, he went to CAP 3-3-5 near Hue City, where he was the CAP leader.

We saw body bags of dead Marines there by the chopper LZ. It was September 1967, my introduction to war.

When I arrived in Vietnam I was assigned to A Company, 9th Engineer Battalion. They were located on Hill 63. At that time there was just our company, some grunts from the 5th Marines, a group from 1st Engineers, a small field [tent] hospital, and an arty battery on the hill. It was exciting being there. I especially liked it when our platoon had the mine sweeps on Highway 1. We would sweep from Hill 63 to the Song Cau Lau Bridge. I really enjoyed trying to talk to the villagers that we passed along the way, although it was usually discouraged. I volunteered to be the platoon's M-60 machine gunner.

In November, the Army's 1st Air Cav started moving into our area and atop Hill 63. Our grunts had left and A Company moved back to our battalion rear at Chu Lai. I felt like a pogue [rear-echelon person] at Chu Lai and wanted to get back into the field. I'd heard some guys talking about CAC units, where Marines went out on operations with the ARVNs, and I thought I'd enjoy doing something like that.

At one of our morning company formations they asked for volunteers for CAC. I raised my hand but two other Marines were chosen. One wanted to go; he was a buddy of mine from West Virginia who was considered by some of the staff NCOs and officers to be a "shitbird." He was reassigned to a CAP, and only a few years ago I found out that he was killed. Another Marine, probably in the same category as my friend, was also persuaded to volunteer.

In January 1968, more volunteers were needed and no one else could be coaxed into it, so they had to take me. On January 20 I went to Da Nang for CAP school. It was right on the beach in East Da Nang, in what looked like an old walled French compound. Just north was Monkey Mountain, and we could see down the beach to the Marble Mountains. The classes were interesting and the chow was good, served by some decent-looking Vietnamese women. My situation seemed to be improving.

The Sunday before the Tet Offensive got under way was a beautiful clear day, one of the first after a never-ending rainy season. That Monday we had classes with several interruptions, one of which was to let us know that the Tet truce had been canceled.

When Da Nang was assaulted on Tuesday morning at 0300, everyone at CAP school was positioned around our perimeter. I was on the beach side. We dug small holes every few feet where there were ports or slits in the walls. It seemed ironic—here we were Marines, in a defensive position against a possible amphibious assault from the NVA or VC. We heard a lot of explosions and firefights around us, plus firecrackers going off. It was difficult to distinguish between the firecrackers and the small-arms fire. We heard reports of lots of CAP units being hit and of other facilities in the Da Nang area coming under attack.

We still had the rest of the week scheduled for school, but the next morning there was a scramble to send us out to the field. I was sent to Golf-5, just south of Da Nang toward Marble Mountain. The Navy Hospital was near this CAP. It was located on a small sandy ridge just west of the north-south road that paralleled the coast. The west side of the ridge sloped off to flat rice-paddy land and the river that flowed toward Da Nang. When I got there they told me the VC and NVA were coming across the river in boats the night before, and enemy soldiers were killed by the CAP and the gunships that were called in.

The CAP leader put us under 100 percent watch that night. I was assigned to a slit trench that faced east toward the road and the beach beyond. It was a cold night with thick fog drifting in off the ocean; I was glad I'd kept my field jacket.

The next morning I volunteered to go out on a patrol. We went down off the river side of the ridge toward some hamlets by the river. Our patrol leader stopped to talk to some villagers and they told him that the VC had carried away many dead and wounded from the previous night attack. We found a lot of bloody rags around the area.

Later a truck came out to get us and took us to MAG-16 at Marble Mountain, where we waited for a chopper to take us to our permanent units. We weren't in the air long when we dropped quickly and landed. Several of us ran off the back of the chopper into a cloud of dust. All I could see was a Marine firing an M-60 from a fighting hole, and I could hear the popping sound of rounds coming in. Someone called to us to get back on the chopper. Ammo and C-rations were kicked off as we scrambled back on board. When we landed again, three of us were told to get off.

My CAP was Delta-1, which looked like an old crumbling French fortification. It was on the east side of Highway 1, next to the Thanh Quit River. I was sent to the north perimeter overlooking the river and told to shoot anything that moved. I wasn't sure who was in charge; several corporals were giving us orders but nobody introduced himself as our CAP leader.

After an hour or so I noticed a Vietnamese man in black trousers, white shirt, and a khaki rain hat, riding a bike across the road from the east to the west side. It seemed odd because I hadn't seen anyone else in the village across the river. I hesitated to shoot because he wasn't a soldier. No one else fired either, so they must've thought as I did or didn't even see him. About fifteen minutes later we took some B-40s from the area he'd gone into. One hit about fifteen feet from me, just on the other side of a small sandbagged shed. One of the Marines who'd arrived with me that day took a direct hit and was killed instantly. I can't remember his name, but he was from Kentucky. Another round hit the Vietnamese CP directly behind us.

At this particular CAP we didn't have PFs, we had RFs. Our AO included the villages of Thanh Quit 1 and 2, north of the river, Thanh Quit 4, Phong Ngu 1 and 2, Quang Loc Tay 3, and An Thanh, on the south side. With the exception of adjacent parts of Phong Ngu, sympathies seemed to be on the side of the VC.

Recollections of my first few weeks there are like a big blur today. People coming and going, KIAs, WIAs, replacements. Plus an assortment of CAP leaders in a short time. Korean and American Marines stayed in our compound sometimes. I recall a short artillery round hitting some of our own grunts in our compound.

The Korean Marines wiped out a hamlet just south of us called Phong Nhi, after they took some sniper fire from the hamlet. This was near our sister CAP Delta-2. The villagers in our area hated the Koreans. Some months later, after I knew the language better, an old lady came up to me and said we should fight the Koreans,

Tom Harvey (second from right)

not the Vietnamese. Other villagers asked why we couldn't get the Koreans to leave Vietnam.

Later I learned that our CACO commander, Lieutenant Sylvia, complained all the way up the line to Saigon about the incident at Phong Nhi, but all that ever came out of it was he got transferred to the Charlie CAPs out in Dai Loc District to guard against possible threats on his life. It's only been in later years that I read about the incident at Phong Nhi in Guenter Lewy's *America in Vietnam* (1978).

On February 13, 1968, a wounded Marine came staggering into our compound—William Tallaferro. He'd been taken prisoner after being hit in a firefight while on patrol at our sister CAP Delta-3. He was an FO [forward observer] with Kilo Company, 3d Battalion, 5th Marines. He told us that the NVA were using young kids as ammo humpers. They'd left him for dead after they were subjected to repeated air and arty strikes. He'd received numerous wounds, was extremely thin, and looked and smelled terrible, although we weren't too clean or pretty ourselves during this time.

Things quieted down a little in March. We finally got a "permanent" CAP leader, too—Sergeant Young. I remembered him from CAP school and was glad to see him. He'd been in recon before coming to CAP. We began regular patrols then. On one patrol I was walking point when we found some NVA gear but didn't make contact. The villagers seemed to be going about their normal business and were not unfriendly toward us, which was a good sign.

The next patrol was into An Thanh. Several of us didn't like the idea, because the last patrol into that area had gotten hit pretty bad. Our patrol consisted of five or six Marines and a couple of RFs. Young told me to take the point but a guy named Red, a short-timer, said, "He walked point last time, I'll take it."

We started moving across the open area between Phong Ngu and An Thanh. I saw a farmer with a hoe start to run but before I could think of how to react, we took fire from the tree line ahead of us.

It all happened so fast. Young hollered, "Red's down!" A black Marine named White ran up and screamed, "Where's Red? Where's Red?" Young pointed to where he was lying and White ran to him. He'd been shot in the chest and we called in a medevac chopper. It seemed like forever. Red said, "Please get me out of here, I'm going to die." He was still alive but we heard he died that same day on the operating table.

I never thought about it for a long time. I didn't want to think about it, but Red died for me.

When the dry season came in early April and the weather warmed up, we washed and swam in the river next to our compound. The ground in our compound was so hard you couldn't get a pick into it. Dirt and timber were brought in for us to improve our bunkers and fighting holes. Engineers built a couple of bunkers for us, too. Our compound was small, roughly 200 by 150 feet. Only portions of the old French walls remained, and they were no more than four feet high. The most striking feature about our place was the fifty-five-foot tower that stood near the center of the compound.

Our weapons were assorted. The RFs had mostly World War II–vintage arms: M-1 Garands, M-2 carbines, BARs, and grease guns. We had our M-16s, M-79s, two M-60 machine guns, and a .50-caliber machine gun.

We got along well with our RFs. I trusted them in a firefight and became close friends with some of them. One especially was a favorite among the Marines, a real joker and comic. He'd do a dance routine when they were called out into their evening formation. Sometimes we ate with them; we bought crabs or some other local food at the market across the river in Thanh Quit, a welcome change from C-rations.

In the evenings from our tower, with a telescope, we frequently saw VC equipped with packs and rifles walking out beyond An Thanh to the west of our CAP, and out along the far side of the

Vinh Dien River to our east. We reported these sightings and sometimes called in arty missions on them. It became standard practice to have us go out and check the results of these arty missions. Due to the distance, though, we stopped calling in arty. We had a very small number of people, and it was very dark by the time we reached the area, so we just watched them.

Our compound was never overrun while I was there, but we did get hit frequently at night, usually with small arms and B-40 rockets. They also had an M-79 [40-mm grenade launcher] with them and someone knew how to use it.

The bridge over the river had been blown by the enemy during the Tet Offensive, and a contingent from the 7th Engineer Battalion came to rebuild it. The first night, they stayed in the compound with us. It was just getting dark and they were standing around laughing and joking, when we got hit with the usual stuff. After that they never stayed with us; they went back to Da Nang every evening.

Our CAP was sometimes used as a blocking force during sweep operations by other units. On one of these sweeps, the Korean Marines were coming toward us. We were set up, along with Delta-2 and Delta-3, along the west side of the Song Vinh Dien. For some reason, when the Koreans saw us they opened up. Maybe it was because we had PFs and RFs with us, I'll never know. Anyway, it took a long time to go through all the various communications to get them to lift their fire. We were all lying face down in the dry paddies, and luckily nobody from our CAP was hurt. However, there were some KIAs and WIAs in Delta-2 and Delta-3. I saw one of the Marines from Delta-2 raise his arm and shake it, cursing the Koreans.

After Tet, the 27th Marines came into our AO. Sometimes one or two of our CAP personnel acted as guides for them. Temperatures of 110 degrees were common during the dry season, and one hot day a couple of us were escorting elements of the 27th Marines to the Song Vinh Dien. We had to cross a large paddy that had dried out; there were large clumps of earth that had hardened like bricks. It was extremely tough to walk through this. Their officers and NCOs were screaming, "Don't walk on the paddy dikes!" They were afraid of booby traps, but we had come to feel almost at home in this particular area. Judging from the villagers' behavior, we felt confident that there was no problem, so we walked the dikes ourselves. After this the grunts lined up in formation, standing at attention in the scorching heat with their gas masks on, while their officers and staff NCOs chewed them out for wanting to walk on the dikes. Our RFs watched in disbelief as we witnessed one more reason we were happy to be in a CAP.

On another one of these operations out by the Song Vinh Dien, we discovered some fresh graves and asked the locals who was buried there. They told us they'd buried some NVA soldiers. We asked an old lady, as she served us tea, if she would bury us if we were killed. She said no. She said she'd "throw us in the river and feed us to the fish." We all had a good laugh over that.

Sometime in April or May 1968, I'd just finished cleaning my rifle and was walking across the compound when I saw a jet diving down on us. I saw the fins open on two bombs that were coming right for us. It was a terrifying feeling. I dove into a bunker and thought, Damn! the NVA have planes now. I sure hope they don't come back. The bombs hit about twenty feet outside our compound, on the east side of the road. Most of the shrapnel went into Phong Ngu, severely wounding one old woman and inflicting minor wounds on other villagers.

The woman with the serious wound was brought in by her family. She had a large piece of hot jagged steel completely imbedded in her backside. We called a medevac chopper for her but her family pleaded with us not to send her away. They kept saying, "Chet roi, Chet roi." That means she's already dead or going to die anyway. We thought she had a chance and had her sent to the hospital against her family's wishes, but we later found out that she did die. Her family returned, telling us, "See . . . we told you she was already dead."

We also learned what had happened. One of our Marines had thrown a Willie Peter [white phosphorous] grenade out into the old French minefield next to the road where it passed our compound, attempting to burn off some tall weeds. At the same time, an air strike was in progress about 1,500 meters to our east, and they were using spotter planes and Willie Peter to mark targets for the jets. Those two bombs were right on our smoke. Luckily one turned out to be a dud and skidded about 500 meters into Phong Ngu. Da Nang wanted the bomb back and we were ordered to retrieve it. We couldn't lift and carry the thing, but four of our RFs, none of whom weighed over 120 pounds, came out and rigged it up with bamboo poles and rope. They carried it out to the road and never set it down once. A truck arrived from Da Nang and took it away.

The villagers asked us why we'd called the bombs on them, and I tried to explain in my best Vietnamese that it was mistake. But it was an unfortunate incident that didn't help our relationship with the villagers.

We also had RDs [Revolutionary Development Cadres] in our compound for a while. Many of them were city kids, much more sophisticated than our RFs. One was an older man, very serious, who told me he'd fought with the Viet Minh in the French war.

One night we got hit with small-arms fire. The VC set up loudspeakers and started talking, attempting to coax the RDs and RFs into turning against us and joining them. Our first reaction was to yell obscenities at them in both languages, but this former Viet Minh soldier said no, that would make us look bad in the eyes of the villagers. I really liked that RD and learned from him. Wish I would have had more time to get to know him.

By June Sergeant Young was gone. We got a new CAP leader, Sergeant Bailey. Late one morning, Delta-3 made contact with a VC platoon and requested help. Delta-2 sent some people and Lightning-1, the mobile reaction force from CACO Headquarters, also went.

Bailey told me to get my squad together. Our squads were comprised of four or five Marines and as many RFs as we could muster; usually three or four. We went by truck to Delta-3, which was a bad area. It was situated just north of Go Noi Island in a place we referred to as Dodge City.

We pursued the VC platoon north and west of Delta-3's compound, taking sporadic fire from distant tree lines as we progressed. It was nothing serious; the area was mostly overgrown fields and abandoned houses. Finally we arrived at a VC ville, very much like the one we'd used in training while going through staging at Camp Pendleton. The entrance was a wooden gate that had a big wood VC star on it. There were smoldering fires, ammo, clothing, and 782 gear [helmet, canteen, cartridge belt, and similar items] everywhere. There was also the hulk of a U.S. plane laying there. Narrow zigzag trenches were scattered throughout the place, mostly at the base of rows of bamboo trees. Cleverly hidden. We were almost on top of them before we saw them. As we started toward the next tree line the firing became more intense and one of the PFs was shot through the neck. A medevac chopper came out, one of those old CH-34s, and it too received heavy fire. It must have been hit several more times, because we heard on the radio that it autorotated [went down due to loss of power] near Highway 1.

Later that year Sierra-3 near Hoi An was overrun, and everyone was killed except one wounded Marine.

I left Delta-1 in July 1968 after doing a ten-month tour. It was good to be getting out of a dangerous situation, but there was also a surprising feeling of regret to be leaving something I'd come to enjoy more than anything I'd ever done in my life. I also felt bad about leaving buddies and villagers with whom I'd become friends. I knew I'd probably never see these people again, which brought on a feeling of sadness that surprised me in its strength and duration. I'd become accustomed to allowing myself to feel very little emotion.

When I joined the Corps I had aspirations of going to OCS [Officer's Candidate School], but slots were filled when I enlisted and the local draft board was hot on my tail. I had to wait until my first permanent-duty station to apply, which was at Hill 63 with the 9th Engineers. When I got into the Combined Action Program I had second thoughts about becoming an officer and regretted having applied. But my family was anxious for me to attend OCS, so I accepted orders to go and be in a class that began in late July 1968. I didn't do well and had thoughts only of getting back in a CAP. I DOR'd [dropped on request] after about six weeks and signed a waiver a few months later to go back to 'Nam.

I arrived in May 1969 and got as far as III MAF Headquarters in Da Nang before learning that I was being kept there to work in a carpentry shop. It took me all summer to get back into CAP.

In September 1969 I'd completed the two-week course and was assigned as CAP leader at CAP 3-3-5 in Phu Thu District, east of Hue. There was only one hamlet in our TAOR—Ba Lang. We had PFs there and a good Trung-si. The original village had been destroyed and Ba Lang was a collection of sheet metal and thatched huts laid out in rows in a low-lying area next to a lagoon. To the west was a tree line where the original village had been. It was a tangle of overgrown brush, banana trees, bamboo thickets, the rubble of old masonry homes, hidden VC bunkers, and booby traps. Beyond this the land sloped up to a wasteland of sand dunes and pine trees that stretched to more fertile land around the district headquarters at Phu Thu. The Trung-si told me there were

Tet
1968

80

only local guerrillas here and he knew of no large units in our TAOR.

It was easy to make friends among the people of Ba Lang, but I'm not sure how many of them supported us philosophically. By this time my Vietnamese had improved to the point where I could carry on a small conversation with ease. Our PFs were not from Ba Lang but from other nearby hamlets in Phu Thu District. They could walk through the hamlet and point out things and say this family had two sons with the VC, or that family had a son with the GVN. Sometimes families had sons on both sides. One little girl, five or six years old, had a father who the PFs told us was a honcho with the VC. One day one of our guys started teasing her about that and she cried.

In October 1969 we were hit by a tremendous typhoon. I think we had about seventy-two inches of rain that month. Twenty-two fell in one day, and everything was flooded. We got a couple of kills during that time in spite of the weather, on the back side of the tree line near the sand dunes.

I had one serious falling out with my Trung-si counterpart. One night after the PFs had gotten paid and were planning one of their all-night card games, there was a full moon—not the kind of night we normally would detect any VC movement. I insisted on an ambush at a nice spot I'd found overlooking a gap through the dunes, which made a natural trail into the flat rice lands. My counterpart reluctantly gave us some PFs, and when I found one of them asleep when it came time to "break Buddha" [leave], I got so mad I collected everyone else and left him there asleep.

On the way back the PFs realized someone was missing and started firing their M-16s in the air, hollering for the sleeping PF. This was about 0200 hours. When we got back to Ba Lang I was furious and took it out on the Trung-si. I realized later how stupid I was, but it was too late. My counterpart said he would have me transferred. I didn't think he had that kind of power and forgot about it.

The next morning I got a call on the radio from CACO Head-quarters to have my gear packed and meet the mail jeep later that day. The company gunny was in the jeep and asked me what happened and if I wanted to leave. I told him I wanted to stay, and he said, "Go ahead and stay with your unit, I'll take care of it." Later I apologized to the Trung-si and we worked well together through the rest of my tour there.

We had a Kit Carson scout, a young kid the VC had captured during the Tet Offensive near Hue. He was made to follow them around but Chieu Hoi'd [gave himself up] at his first opportunity. He'd attended the Kit Carson School at Quang Tri.

One morning our patrol was out in the dunes near the boundary with CAP 3-3-3. Usually we avoided these border areas so as not to mistake a friendly patrol for VC. We were looking around the remains of an old compound on the ridge at the eastern edge of the dunes. There was a heavy dew that morning and we could see where some of it had been shaken off of the tall grass. The spoor led down over the hill, and at the bottom we saw some air vents in the ground, and our Kit Carson scout spotted a well-camouflaged trapdoor. We opened it and there were two VC hiding inside. They came out without a fight. They were young, just local guerrillas. We captured two AK-47s and a rusty old M-16. They also had a radio and a parachute flare off of an illumination arty round. One of them had a photo in his wallet of one of the young ladies in Ba Lang, the pretty widow of one of our PFs who'd been killed by a booby trap while on patrol with us a month earlier. We had her taken in to district headquarters for questioning, but she was released later that same day. That night we ambushed another bunker our captives told us about, but we came up empty-handed.

By late 1969 most of our grunts from the 3d Marine Division had already left. The Army's 101st Airborne had come into our TAOR and had conducted a few operations. Our relations with them were not so good; their presence relieved us of having to go out on night ambushes, but they still caused problems. They burned some of our villagers' haystacks, killed a fourteen-year-old boy, and took other villagers in as VC suspects. Once a stray bullet killed a baby nursing at its mother's breast while they were fam [familiarization] firing their weapons. I began to relate to the villagers more and more and could see what they had to go through day by day.

In December I grew very weak with alternating chills and extreme fever plus bloody stool. Finally I was medevaced to the hospital in Phu Bai for dysentery for about ten days.

After the first of the year I returned and we moved south to the hamlet of Luong Vien. Our PFs had moved before us and had already made contact and killed one VC. We were anxious to get in a new AO. On our first patrol two Marines, Rob Olson and an Indian we called Chief, tripped a couple of daisy-chained [tied together] booby-trapped U.S. M-26 grenades. They were both seriously wounded. Olson and I had been close and I felt terrible, because I'd been called back to Phu Bai that day. Olson was expected to live but was going to lose both legs; Chief was expected to recover after several months in the hospital. But late in the evening we received a call over the radio. Olson did not survive.

We kept up aggressive patrolling and got several more kills, all local VC. We initiated a program to deny booby-trap material to the VC: we made payment to people, mostly kids, who brought in hundreds of pounds of dud ordnance. I still have my notebook with a list of all the names of the VC known to have been in our AO.

We began hearing rumors that we were going to be deactivated, and by mid-March we knew for certain that we would leave early. I left Vietnam on Easter Sunday, March 31, 1970. My feelings were mixed, again. It was good to get out of the field with the prospect of going home and seeing family and friends, but there were also friends in Ba Lang and Luong Vien, and the thought of never seeing them again made me very sad.

It's hard to say how successful we were in Vietnam, but I think there was a big variation from unit to unit, from location to location, and from time period to time period. I think the concept of CAP was one of the best to come out of the U.S. effort in Vietnam, and one of the few that wasn't counterproductive. But I don't think it was anywhere near enough to overcome the VC. We had no political training at all and there was no way we could compete with the VC in that area, even when we were teamed with a group of good PFs. On a personal level, some of the CAPs accomplished a lot toward a better understanding between the Vietnamese and the Americans. But I think our other military efforts only worsened an already bad political climate, which in the end made victory impossible for us. Our leaders gauged success on statistics, which in Vietnam was senseless.

In 1989 I went back to Vietnam with eight CAP Marines. We wanted to see what had become of "our villages." Through the years a lot of bitterness had built up inside of me, toward the communists, our government policy makers, the antiwar protestors, the media, and the general attitude of most Americans who couldn't care less about what happened in Southeast Asia. I wasn't sure how I'd handle a trip back there; I had reservations right up to departure time.

But the welcome we got from the people in Vietnam, even in the north, was much better than anything we'd experienced on our return to the States. I did make it back to Ba Lang, where I met the two former VC who I'd helped take prisoner in November 1969. The welcome there completely wrung me out emotionally and beyond anything I can put into words. It was totally spontaneous. I went there with one other former CAP Marine. We had no guide, and nobody from Vietnam Tourism had any idea where Ba Lang was located. No one knew we were coming. Luong Vien was three kilometers down the trail, but we didn't have time to visit. I still hope to go someday.

It was dusk when we left Ba Lang and headed back to Hue. Twenty years earlier we would have been moving into our night position. It gave me an eerie sensation of déjà vu, although I felt a tremendous sense of relief that we didn't have to do it anymore. I remarked to Phil Ovelman, who was with me, what a fine welcome it had been. "Yeah," he said, "I wonder what it would've been like if we would've won?"

Since my trip the bitterness has subsided somewhat, except for toward our leaders who got us involved in the first place and then pulled the plug. I've located my former Trung-si counterpart from 3-3-5. He did ten years in a reeducation camp after being taken in 1975. Now there's a good chance he'll come to the U.S. under the Orderly Departure Program.

I've also been in touch with a village girl I used to see and talk with at the market in Thanh Quit. Of course she's older now and has a family. She told me the war had been a nightmare for her village, and her uncle had fought against our CAP. It's obvious from her letters that she also sympathized with the VC. But she, and so many others we met, have put the war behind them and seem to have some difficulty understanding why we Americans can't do the same. She says she hopes that relations between our countries will soon be such that my family can visit her home. I hope so too.

*　　*　　*

Tom Harvey lives near Millboro, Virginia, where he is a shift supervisor in the operations department at an electric power plant in the mountains of Bath County. In his spare time he does volunteer work teaching English to Vietnamese refugees in Roanoke and is a member of the CAP Unit Veterans Association. He publishes their quarterly newsletter, CAPNEWS. Tom dreams of someday returning to Vietnam to make a contribution toward rebuilding the country.

B. Keith Cossey

2d CAG
1966–1968

B. Keith Cossey served in Echo-4, Foxtrot-2, and Golf-4 CAPs during his two tours in Vietnam. In addition to being a squad leader, he was selected to be a member of a multinational advisory team at 2d CAG District Headquarters in Da Nang.

I was a squad leader and adviser to one of the Golf series of CAP outposts near Da Nang in the spring of 1968. Our platoon was digging a trench around our compound, which consisted of an abandoned Buddhist temple and Seabee-built huts. The village chief and the local PFs had told us not to dig in one certain area, an area that was tactically important to our defenses.

It was a gnarled old sacred tree. We were told it would be sacrilegious to desecrate the ground with a pick or shovel anywhere in the shadow of the tree. We didn't want to insult the villagers, but we also didn't want to leave a vital sector of our perimeter open to possible enemy intrusion. What we finally did was build an above-ground wall of sandbags on the holy ground, so we didn't have to dig.

Late in my second tour of duty, I was brought back from the bush and assigned to a district headquarters as a member of a multinational advisory team composed of CAP Marines, an Australian or two, some U.S. Army types, a Navy corpsman, and a number of South Vietnamese officers and men.

One day a Korean soldier was shopping in the village and talking with a young Vietnamese woman who'd just sold him some cigarettes. A group of ARVNs happened along and sternly told him that he was not to fraternize with "one of our women." The Korean ignored them. One of the ARVNs fired his M-16 at the Korean's feet to scare him. The Korean took out his pistol, shot his tormentor dead, and kept talking to the lady.

A mixed mob of soldiers and civilians brought the Korean into the district headquarters for "justice." They planned to lynch him, but our advisory team managed to confine the prisoner in a building away from the developing riot. One Vietnamese man broke through our guard, though, and gave the Korean a flesh wound with a bayonet. It became obvious that we could not give him adequate protection under the explosive circumstances.

We decided to transport the prisoner to Da Nang, where the headquarters for the Korean troops was located. There he could be taken into custody and eventually given a military trial.

But how to do it? The district headquarters was surrounded by an ever-growing armed mob.

We figured the ARVNs and their rabble of accomplices would be hesitant to open fire on Americans, so we carefully backed a jeep through the crowd and parked it right inside the building. We put the Korean on the back of the jeep's open floor; unfortunately there was no protective canvas or upper body of the vehicle. I had to literally sit on the prisoner and face to the rear with my M-16 off safe. Another CAP Marine drove. A long driveway, maybe 100 meters, stretched between our building and the open highway. All along it, ARVNs and local militiamen had their rifles pointed at us.

The driver started the jeep and pulled out fast, scattering the people attempting to block our departure. Then we drove slowly and deliberately between the scowling ranks of armed men, with our faces in their rifle sights.

After turning onto the highway, we hauled ass all the way to Da Nang.

Just before the 1968 Tet Offensive, a friend from another CAP outpost, a lance corporal, came to visit me at my CAP, Echo-4, in the village of Lo Giang. I needed company.

For a week or more our village had suddenly been filled with strange young men in civilian clothes. No one had ever seen them before, but each one carried a South Vietnamese ID card. We took in for questioning those who had obviously forged credentials, but we had our hands full with literally hundreds of these characters just hanging around. We didn't realize that the 1st NVA Regiment had selected our turf as a staging area for its upcoming assault on Da Nang, which was twelve to fifteen miles away.

During my friend's visit we noticed a kid crouched under a tree, very skinny and looking exhausted. He was too young to be potentially harmful, maybe eleven or twelve, so we invited him inside

B. Keith Cossey

our fortified compound to have some food and a sheltered place to sleep before moving on. Marines were always suckers for orphans. Technically we weren't supposed to let them inside our defenses but what the heck, every Marine was a bit of a bastard himself.

A week or two later all hell broke loose as the enemy violated the Tet holiday truce and unleashed massive attacks all over Vietnam. We were not spared. Our CAP was directly in the path of the NVA drive toward Da Nang. Terribly outnumbered and surrounded, we tried to hold our positions and survive until the Army's American Division could send elements from down south to seal the open countryside between us and Da Nang.

Nineteen men from other CAP outposts in the area—both Marines and PFs—volunteered to attack the flank of the NVA battalion that was decimating us at Echo-4. This small reaction force could not hope to overwhelm the enemy, but they just might distract them long enough to buy us some time to regroup, patch up our wounded, and hold on. One of the nineteen volunteers was my friend.

At first the NVA unit tried to ignore this reinforced squad ripping away at their flanks and concentrated on our village. Failing to overrun our compound, they turned their fury on the small band of brave volunteers, led by Capt. Howard Joselane, USMC.

American fighter pilots overhead refused to fire on the enemy as they swarmed out of the tree line to engulf the squad. The pilots could not believe that these hundreds of Vietnamese running around on the ground wearing helmets, uniforms, and camouflage could be anything but a friendly regiment of ARVNs just arrived to reinforce us.

Seventeen out of the nineteen volunteers were killed. Only two survived: Corporal Talbot and my friend. My friend, wounded by shrapnel, was on the ground trying to help another CAP friend of ours who was choking to death after having been shot in the throat. An NVA soldier came from behind and bayoneted them both. When he regained consciousness, my friend saw that he was the only American left alive.

The NVA were torturing to death the South Vietnamese PFs. An NVA soldier spotted my friend moving and motioned to the others he'd go over and kill him. But then an NVA radioman ran over and intercepted the other soldier, gesturing that he'd do the job for him.

The fully helmeted and uniformed radio operator came and stood over my friend. It was the kid we'd befriended a week or two previously.

The kid motioned for him to lay his head down and pointed his rifle at him. At least, my friend thought, he's going to make it short and sweet and is not going to screw with me like his buddies are with the PFs. The kid then fired next to his head purposely and strode off to report that he had accomplished his mission.

That act of kindness we had performed earlier had saved my friend's life.

*   *   *

B. Keith Cossey graduated "with highest honors" from Norwich University in Vermont in 1973. He has undergone lengthy counseling for post-traumatic stress disorder. He recently completed a novel for young adults, "Temporary Manhood," which chronicles the misadventures of a group of high-schoolers invited to go along on a U.S. Marine Corps Reserve drill weekend. He lives in Carey, Ohio, with his family.

Tom Krusewski

3d CAG
1967–1968

After a stint with Company H, 2d Battalion, 26th Marines, Tom Krusewski volunteered for a CAP unit. He was assigned to Hotel CAPs near Hue City. In January 1968, Hotel-6 was overrun by elements of an NVA regiment poised to strike Hue City during the Tet Offensive.

About four o'clock in the morning on January 7, 1968, we woke up to the sound of mortar and recoilless rifle fire. Sapper squads had penetrated the compound; we only had a couple of guys out on bridge security. Hotel-6 was being overrun.

I'd been in country for about two and half months when I was transferred to a CAP from 26th Marines. I used to ride by it along Highway 1. Another Marine, Arliss Willhite, went to CAP Hotel-6 with me. This was at the end of September or beginning of October 1967.

Hotel-6 was semi-new, in the village of Nuoc Ngot, south of Phu Bai. It was a nice village, thinking back on it—too nice.

They were still building the compound when we arrived. It wasn't very big, and it was oval-shaped—about 200 feet across and 150 feet wide.

I think every CAP compound was incorrectly built and incorrectly located. They made it look like a fortress, so it was an easy target. There was an old French fort about 400 yards away. We had big giant bunkers and lookout towers—how could they miss! We had these four giant towers that were leveled by B-40 rockets the night we were overrun.

When I look back on it I think, How stupid could our officers have been? They should have built something that kept a low profile. They taught us at ITR [Infantry Training Regiment] about staying off the horizon, and here they were putting us on one!

We got there and met all the guys and the PFs. We were shakin' because we didn't know what to make of the PFs. As it turned out, they were good. You'll hear stories from other CAP Marines about how bad their PFs were, but ours were okay. Their weapons were old M-1s. The biggest fault they found with us was the fact we got to go home after thirteen months and they had to stay there. They felt it was unfair. But they still thanked us for the year.

I remember the first couple of nights at Hotel-6 we went on bridge security—the gooks kept blowin' this bridge nearby. The first three consecutive nights we scored a kill.

We got along really well with the Vietnamese. We got involved in a lot of civic action, and the corpsmen taught health and hygiene. We also taught the people how to defend their ville.

One of the guys killed the night we were overrun was Tiny Nielsen, related to the Nielsens who do the TV ratings. He'd asked his uncle for a swing set for the village, and it came after he died. Little things like that meant a lot.

In November the villagers threw a big Christmas party, complete with a big feast. They strung lanterns down the pathway for us. That was nice. I still have pictures of it. There were quite a few orphans; nearby was an orphanage run by some Catholic nuns.

It was real tough eating some of their food, but you did it to keep their trust. You never slapped them around like some of the grunts in regular units. During Tet, though, the villagers wouldn't feed us even though we weren't getting any supplies. In all fairness, the NVA were probably stealing their rice and they didn't have any to give to us. We stole bags of rice off the South Vietnamese civilian trucks going to market. We even ate the compound dog, that's how tough it got.

One real rainy night in November, John Calhoun and his bunch were out on ambush. They watched for about an hour as an NVA battalion walked right in front of them. They called in Puff, but the gunship couldn't find them because of the heavy downpour. We think that was the NVA force that came back through in January to get us. We'd been challenged in the village, so Willhite and myself put signs up saying Come and Get Us. They had a price on our heads—not very much, though. We didn't make the big time.

They also dropped leaflets. Our government dropped them out of planes, but the NVA dropped them on the trails for us to find. The leaflets showed a picture of a nice blonde babe wearing a lot of lipstick and makeup, saying, "Will they return home safely? Merry Christmas." Sometimes they said, "American black GI, why are you fighting Johnson's war of aggression?" It was psychological warfare, but it was actually funny. Everything was misspelled. And we didn't even have any blacks in Hotel-6. In fact

I don't recall seeing any blacks in the CAPs until after January 1968. During my stay at Hotel-6, we got word that a black Marine or soldier was running with the VC, and that turned out to be true.

It was quiet during November and December 1967. When we sent in reports on that large force we'd seen in November, nobody believed us. That was one of the problems with CAPs—we didn't have any officers with us. They thought we exaggerated. And they distrusted the Vietnamese. Everything in the CAP had to be cleared through district headquarters, where the Vietnamese district chief was located, and he was corrupt and flaunted his riches. Then we were also dealing with this corrupt government in Saigon.

One day we found motorcycle tracks through the jungle, made by those small Hondas the Vietnamese rode around on. They would ride out to pay off the VC. We went on a four-day search for these guys but found nothing. We came back on the night of January 6, and our NCOIC didn't put out any LPs or OPs. He thought we were too tired, and some of the other Marines talked him into not doing it. We had become complacent; there hadn't been any action in our AO for several months. But the enemy was waiting.

Our compound was next to the railroad tracks alongside Highway 1, which provided a natural bunker for the enemy. They attacked right over the railroad tracks in human waves; someone had opened the gates for them and let them in.

We had five hootches made out of plywood, screens, and corrugated-tin roofs. Arliss Willhite and myself were in the last hootch, which is the reason we survived. We used to tie our hootch door shut with comm [communication] wire because the wind blew it open. When they blew the tower, one of the Marines tossed a grenade into the wire and it lit up some of the illum [illumination rounds], and there they were. The sappers threw satchel charges into the hootches where these Marines were sleeping, but when they got to ours the door was wired shut. That saved us.

We got an M-60 set up but the machine gunner was killed. We had very, very, very good PFs. This one guy had a BAR [Browning automatic rifle], and it kept us alive. I can still hear that rifle chattering. I believe he got a high American decoration, I can't remember which one. He didn't die that night, but I'm sure he died later in a reeducation camp because he worked with Americans.

We only had enough time to grab our rifles, cartridge belts, and a few hand grenades. Then we beat feet to our bunker. There were quite a few NVA; we were actually pushing them away! We weren't sure if they were PFs or communists. The sappers had come through first and blown the hootches and were tossing satchel charges everywhere. In fact, seventy-three satchel charges didn't even go off! The VC threw a lot of satchel charges that night. Within half an hour, the entire compound was set on fire.

Also, the gooks had bullhorns hollering at us, "We are going to kill you, Ha-si [Corporal] Willhite. You die Ha-si Ski." They even had the whole village out there cheering!

We had a double squad that night. We had about twenty-five Marines in the compound because of that search we were on, but we still lost twelve KIA that night. We also had two walls they didn't come over that provided us with excellent fields of fire. They cut right through the concertina wire we had around the compound, but in certain sections they couldn't get through. That's because we were drunk when we strung it out; thank God we were drinking that day! We found out later they had a mock compound set up that they practiced assaulting.

That night, three Marines were awarded the Navy Cross— John Calhoun, Robert Rusher, and Claude Dorris. Calhoun went out to save another Marine who was hit in the face by Willie Peter; he never made it back.

It was the 85th NVA Regiment that overran us. One lesson I learned from this was you can't trust your support. The NVA was hitting our other support units at the same time they were attacking us, tying them down. Hotel-7, Hotel-Actual, and the arty battery were also hit.

Bac Ma was a major NVA hospital, and it was only one klick from Nuoc Ngot. It was supposed to be underground and it had a major tunnel system. If you look at the map, it was pretty logical for them to put it there. Right between Da Nang and Hue.

We'd predicted the whole thing, but nobody believed us. We actually predicted the 1968 Tet Offensive, but the information was cut off at the district level and never reached 1st or 3d Marine Division intelligence.

The morning after the attack Colonel Brady came to see us. He didn't say much, just shook his head. He had on his flak jacket, pistol, helmet, the whole bit—and we were standing there in our underwear. During this whole battle we were in our skivvies. In the morning the spotter plane came over, passed over us twice.

The second time he dropped out a pair of utility trousers. To this day I don't know where he got them.

I received some minor shrapnel wounds and we had four emergency medevacs. I never found any of the guys that were taken out on emergency medevacs. The bridge was totally destroyed. We had three Marine MIAs. One guy from Hotel-7 was in the well all night, and the other two were later found.

The hardest part after it was over was identifying the dead. We stayed in Hotel-6. The 5th Marines soon joined us, and we had contact for fourteen straight days in February. We finally left and blew up the compound. Then we pulled back to our headquarters, Hotel-Actual, in Phu Loc. In April we went back and rebuilt the entire Hotel-6 compound.

Later I was in one of the first mobile CAPs, Hotel-10, where I was a CAP leader. The mobile concept seemed to work a little better. Hotel-10 was right where the South China Sea and the Gulf of Tonkin meet. Real pretty, but real hot. We didn't go out on too many patrols while we were there, and if we did we stayed close to Highway 1.

We had a tight group of guys. Capt. James Hall was our CACO commander; he got killed. He was a hell of a guy, I can tell you that. He'd bring us fresh milk in his jeep. He'd drive out to us even though they'd mined Highway 1. He'd be driving down the highway dodging the mines.

I shared the CAP leader position at Hotel-10 with Sgt. Joe Cerrone. He got killed after I left Vietnam in August 1968. Yeah . . . there were quite a few that didn't make it.

★   ★   ★

Tom Krusewski graduated from Southern Connecticut State University with a degree in elementary education. He taught school for three years and is now the projects manager for Whalley Glass Company in New Haven, Connecticut. He is married with three children.

1969–1971
Wind-down

After Tet the Combined Action Program experienced some growth. In July the 4th Combined Action Group, the smallest of the four groups, was formed, its AO in Northern I Corps, a sparsely populated region.

As 1969 approached, there were 102 CAPs in I Corps. By the summer, 114 were in place. The Marine Corps had finally reached its goal—two years behind schedule.

The new year also brought dramatic changes in the overall war. A new policy, dubbed Vietnamization, was being introduced. The ultimate responsibility for the conflict was being slowly handed over to the South Vietnamese. In August 1969 the first U.S. troops were pulled out of Vietnam. By year's end the majority of the 3d Marine Division had been redeployed to Okinawa and Hawaii, and III MAF relinquished control of the CAPs to the U.S. Army's XXIV Corps.

This pullout presented some problems for the CAPs operating in the 3d Marine Division's TAOR, but not all U.S. Army support was looked upon unfavorably. Illustrations of both situations are included in this chapter.

Finally, on January 11, 1970, III MAF established the Combined Action Force (CAF), which incorporated the four CAGs under its own separate headquarters instead of the III MAF assistant chief of staff.

However, with the departure of the 3d Marine Division in late 1969 and the 1st Marine Division by early 1971, III MAF began to dissolve the CAPs. The 4th CAG was first, followed by the 3d, the 1st, and ultimately the 2d. CAP Marines expressed disappointment and downright anger as the regular line units departed Vietnam.

To augment the CAPs as they were winding down, regular line units provided companies to work with the Vietnamese. The U.S.

Army's Americal Division sent Company C, 52d Infantry, and Company D, 46th Infantry. The 1st Marine Division dispatched Company M, 3d Battalion, 1st Marines, followed by Company A, 1st Battalion, 7th Marines, and Company K, 3d Battalion, 26th Marines. This program, first called the Infantry Company Intensive Pacification Program (ICIPP), was redesignated the Combined Unit Pacification Program (CUPP).

The mission of the CUPPs should not be confused with that of the CAPs. Generally, CUPP personnel were not trained in CAP school (although a few did attend), and CUPP units were still under operational control of their parent battalion.

Another important development was the CAP mobile concept. Up until this time CAPs had been garrisoned in compounds. The mobile CAP, the Marines felt, would keep the enemy off balance by not knowing the CAP's whereabouts. Said Col. Theodore E. Metzger, CAF commander, "They don't like to come after you unless they've had a chance to get set and do some planning. Mobility throws this off. . . . The CAP can be found anywhere outside a village or hamlet, and they don't like this when they're trying to come in for rice, or money, or recruits, or just plain coordination" (Cosmas 1986, 145).

But Gene Ferguson, a CAP Marine who served in both compound and mobile CAPs, disagrees. "When I was in the compound, we could scrounge up another M-60 machine gun . . . .50 cal . . . 60 mm mortars . . . diesel fuel with . . . napalm powder in [them] and electric blasting caps. In the mobile CAP they could slaughter us like flies" (Peterson 1989, 61).

As it had been in 1967, the Marine manpower after 1969 was stretched thin. There were great changes within the organization as the CAPs were winding down, yet neither their mission nor the nature of their combat changed.

On May 17, 1971, 2d CAG was officially dissolved, and the Combined Action Program ceased to exist.

On April 3, 1971, while on patrol west of Dien Ban District Headquarters, CAPs 2-3-3 and 2-3-7 came under fire. One Marine was killed, the last CAP Marine to die in Vietnam.

Michael Cousino

2d CAG
1968–1969

Bored with the humdrum life of a rear-echelon Marine, Mike Cousino requested transfer to a CAP. He was assigned to 2d CAG in the Da Nang area and served there until he was seriously wounded in February 1969.

Our war was different from the average grunt's. From what I'd heard, I thought the CAP would be swinging duty. Was I wrong! There were quite a few problems we had to overcome.

There were twelve or thirteen Marines and about thirty PFs. I was the highest-ranking one there, a corporal. The other Marines held the rank of lance corporal or private first class. But we never wore any rank; we always did everything together. We thought and acted as one.

The antiquated weapons and equipment we were given were a problem. We were handed a PRC-10 radio. Can you imagine? We had to actually steal a PRC-25 so we could communicate with our CACO headquarters. The PFs had a wide assortment of weapons: M-1 Garands, BARs, a Thompson submachine gun, .45 caliber pistols. One PF even had a German-made machine pistol. Because of all these different weapons, we had a problem with ammunition. It was funny to watch these little Vietnamese stroll around with their M-1 rifles bigger than they were. I used to wonder if they could reach the trigger when they put the rifle to their shoulder.

Finally we were able to get M-16s for everybody. At least now we could interchange weapons and ammo. I'll tell you though, the M-16s we had were a piece of shit. They jammed half the time if you didn't clean them constantly. Give me an M-14 any day, that was a good weapon. I fired expert with that sucker after boot camp.

Then there was the language barrier. All of us spoke what we called jive Vietnamese. We found this old papa-san who'd served with the French, and he was a great help, spoke English and

French pretty good. We made him head honcho so we could get our PFs' heads and asses wired together.

Finally, we had to train these jokers. What a time that was! What we did was use the show-and-tell method. We showed them how to load a weapon, fire it, clean it properly, all that. Squad tactics was a trip. We had to literally push and shove the PFs around until they got the message. Fortunately we had about two months to train them. It was difficult, but we did it.

Our AO was south of the Ashau Valley, near Happy Valley. I can't understand that one, it wasn't a very happy place to be. We began patrolling the area. One thing that always worried us was our height. We were much taller than the PFs and stuck out like tits on a boar hog. That made us prime targets.

Our first patrol amazed me. Four or five of these PFs are playing radios! So we stopped the patrol, gathered all the radios, and shot the hell out of them!

Our CAP finally got an ARVN interpreter to help us with the language problem. One night this interpreter discovered a PF asleep on perimeter watch—so he cut his throat. Then he woke up all the PFs, took them to the body, and told them he'd cut the throat of any PF he caught sleeping on perimeter watch. We never had another PF fall asleep on us after that.

In a CAP you had to be a jack-of-all-trades. If we encountered a booby trap, we blew it. The same went for tunnels; if you found one, you had to check it out. That was one of my jobs. At that time I weighed 145 pounds, had a 27-inch waist, and was good-looking. So, armed with a .45-caliber pistol and a flashlight, down I'd go. This one time we uncovered a tunnel that ran from the village to the riverbank, a distance of about 500 yards. We actually found it by accident. A Marine checking for hidden weapons inside a hootch knocked over a stove—there it was ! Of course, yours truly went down. We immediately checked all the Vietnamese ID cards and found ten villagers who appeared suspicious. We sent them off to be interrogated.

I still get nightmares about going into those tunnels.

Life in the village was great. We'd relax during the day and watch the villagers working in the rice fields. They had a very primitive life-style. It was peaceful, until one of them stepped on a land mine.

If the papa-san liked you he'd butcher a goat, collect its blood in a bowl, and take a sip. Then he offered it to you. I pretended to drink it by bringing the bowl up to my mouth and letting some

Michael Cousino

blood form around my lips. This way I wouldn't offend him. He accepted me into his family.

The Vietnamese were very superstitious. As Americans, we enjoy patting little kids on the head, but the Vietnamese believe you're putting bad spirits into the child if you do that. If we were sitting down and the heel of my boot was pointing at one of them, that meant that person was going to die the next day.

Sometimes instead of staying in our compound, I stayed in the village all night. I really felt at home there, and I learned to love the Vietnamese people. Back then I thought they were ignorant, but in many ways they weren't. We called the Vietnamese gooks, but in reality we were the gooks. We were foreigners in their land.

I used to amaze the FNGs [fuckin' new guys], especially the ones from the city. I taught them how to hunt, skin animals, build lean-tos, in general how to live off the land. We cooked monkey, snake, dog, even cats. Although I never saw too many cats in Vietnam. I never liked fish too much. To this day I can't stomach rice and fish.

I remember this young Vietnamese kid coming to our compound one evening, just hollering and screaming. He tossed an M-1 rifle over the wire and took off. For six straight nights he repeated this procedure. We couldn't figure out what he was up to. Then, on a day patrol, we found his body, or what was left of it. Finally we found out what he was trying to do. It seems the VC went to his village trying to recruit young men into their ranks. When the village elder refused the VC killed him, quite a few women and kids, and grabbed as many young males as possible for their army. This kid was stealing weapons the VC had hidden in the village and was giving them to us.

Another thing, the VC made it appear that the atrocity was committed by Americans. They left signs all around, like an E-tool or a helmet, so others would think we did it. That was Charlie's PR men at work.

I was wounded on February 10, 1969. I'm disabled as a result and will spend the rest of my life in a wheelchair. There will always be a piece of me in Vietnam.

★   ★   ★

Mike "Wheels" Cousino is a Disabled Veterans Outreach Program Specialist for the New York State Department of Labor. He lives in upstate New York with his wife and three children.

Wind-down
1969–1971

100

Skip Freeman

1st CAG
1969–1970

Before assignment to a CAP unit, Skip Freeman was a machine gunner with Company B, 1st Battalion, 9th Marines, and participated in Operation Dewey Canyon. While serving with CAPs 1-1-1, 1-1-6, and 1-1-7, he was wounded on two occasions.

I was sitting in an old concrete schoolhouse cleaning my M-16. All of a sudden a little five-year-old Vietnamese girl comes running down the dirt road yelling, "VC! VC!" A platoon of NVA was attempting to surround the schoolhouse, and there were only eight or nine of us.

The NVA had cut us off from three sides. So the only thing we could do was run. L. Cpl. Ken Southards was manning our M-60. He jumped out the front door and let loose fifteen- to twenty-round bursts to keep their heads down. Then an NVA soldier jumped out and fired a whole magazine from his AK-47. It was like a duel—a western showdown.

Before we skyed [ran], our radio operator shot the PRC-25 field radio full of holes. We went out the back window and ran across the rice paddies toward Highway 1. That was a close call.

This incident occurred while I was in CAP 1-1-6. We were north of Chu Lai, outside the district capital and northwest of Tam Ky. It was a very hot area. There was a little ville called Ky My—we nicknamed it Kill Me. We were kicked out of the ville on two occasions by NVA and VC. It was so bad they put tanks and APCs [armored personnel carriers] from the Army there with us. The NVA used this area as a resupply route.

The PFs we had at 1-1-6 were very dependable. They wouldn't di-di [run away] like others did. We ran a lot of night patrols and ambushes and took mortar rounds in the compound every night, and we always traveled in pairs. We wouldn't even go to the ville or take a shower unless there were two or three of us. We always covered each others' backs.

Skip Freeman

Some of the other CAPs in the vicinity were having problems. I was transferred from 1-1-6 to 1-1-7 because the entire platoon had been wounded in a firefight, so they took a few of us from other CAPs to reorganize and form a new one. CAP 1-1-7 was located on the east side of Highway 1. It was real sandy, close to the South China Sea. I can't recall the name of the ville, but I can tell you it was a real bad place.

The platoon used Vietnamese mercenaries called Biet Laps. They were hard-core. One of them had five cigarette burns on his arm for each member of his family killed by the VC. When we went on patrol with these guys, we had nothing to worry about. The Biet Laps were paid by a rich Vietnamese lady who lived in Tam Ky. They were organized into four or five companies throughout Quang Tin Province and took their orders from the province chief, through this rich woman.

On one operation an entire company of these Biet Laps went with us. We headed toward the South China Sea, me humping an M-60. I was never so tired in my life humping that thing through the deep sand. Our group was ambushed and pinned down by a sniper who was outstanding. We called in an air strike and an Australian plane dropped 500-pound bombs on the enemy positions. When we swept through the area the sniper was still there. The Biet Laps tried like hell to flush out this sniper and two of them got hit in the head, but that didn't stop them. They didn't slow down a bit. I don't think they found that sniper though. The VC must've crawled into some spider holes.

One day the NVA shot an old man in the foot and made him hobble all the way to our compound about a half-mile away to tell us that they were there and to come and get them. We took a couple of squads of Biet Laps to clean out the ville. It was one hell of a firefight: a couple of Marines and Vietnamese were wounded. We scored six or seven kills, and the NVA eventually cleared out. I think it was all a trick to see how many Marines and Biet Laps were in the area.

I went on R and R and when I returned I found out I'd been transferred again. This time I went to CAP 1-1-1, or what we called Trip 1. That's when I met a Marine named Jerry Shine. We became good friends and I still see him today. We were both lance corporals, but Jerry had been in the CAP longer than me. When Sergeant Prince stepped on a booby trap and was medevaced out, Jerry took over as CAP leader.

Trip 1 was in a little ville called Phu Tra, outside of Tam Ky. We had some bad PFs, in fact there were instances of PFs running and Marines getting killed because of it.

For some reason the high command combined us with CAP 1-1-4 out in the boonies to build a compound. And when I say the boonies, I mean the boonies.

We'd been in the area for about a week and a half when Jerry stepped on a booby-trapped 155-mm round. I was wounded in the explosion and so was Lance Corporal Cantu. Jerry lost both his legs.

Not too long after we finished our compound, which was nothing more than a few bunkers and fighting holes, we started getting hit pretty bad. The nearest ville to our compound was Phu Tra 2. The people seemed pretty nice, but of course they're going to be nice to anyone carrying a gun. I'm sure when the VC or NVA came through they were nice to them too. The villagers charged us sixty cents a beer, and the VC probably took the money.

They split us up again, and CAP 1-1-4 moved on and we stayed in the Phu Tra 2 area. That's when 1-1-4 ran into a lot of trouble. One of my good friends, Pete Gruca, was killed because 1-1-4's PFs ran. They were out on patrol and I was monitoring the radio for Trip 1. Pfc Wesley Sidener called in a fire mission and the South Vietnamese wouldn't clear it because it was near a friendly ville. But NVA were coming out of this so-called friendly ville.

Sidener was on the radio yelling, "I'm hit! I'm hit!" We could hear firing in the background, and that's the last we heard from him. Then we heard Vietnamese voices, not the PFs. Three Marines were killed on that patrol—Gruca, Sidener, plus a Navy corpsman, Hn3c. Gerald Edward Kessling. Two others were wounded, and two PFs died—the Trung-si and his radioman. The rest skyed.

While I was assigned to CAP 1-1-7, we got some tools for the farmers and dug two concrete water wells. It was a very poor village and they had terrible drinking water. They really appreciated the well. We also brought in a naval dental team because the villagers had real bad teeth. They stayed in the ville for two days.

When we first arrived in this ville, a little girl kept saying, "Marines, number ten!" Later, after we helped them, it was, "Marines, number one!"

We were invited to village Tet parties and sometimes we even received some good intelligence because of what we did for them. A cute little ten-year-old kid we called Bobby acted as our interpreter. I was only eight years older than him. I have a picture of him in my house; I can still see him smoking a cigarette.

Before joining a CAP unit I was with Bravo Company, 1st Battalion, 9th Marines. I felt a lot safer in a grunt line company. In the CAP, with only eight or nine guys, you had to really be on your guard. I don't think I'd want to do it again, but I wouldn't trade my Vietnam experience for the world. I tried my best to help the Vietnamese people.

★   ★   ★

Skip Freeman works for the Department of Defense as a production control coordinator at the Naval Aviation Depot, Cherry Point, North Carolina. He is married with two daughters.

Col. Edward F. Danowitz, USMC (Ret.)

Director, Combined Action Program
1968–1969

Commissioned a 2d lieutenant in the Marine Corps in 1942, Col. Edward F. Danowitz is a veteran of World War II, Korea, and Vietnam. He took over as Director, Combined Action Program, in October 1968. He remained in this capacity until April 8, 1969, when he was reassigned as commanding officer of the 9th Marines.

My capacity was assistant chief of staff of III MAF and director of the four CAGs. While I headed the program, I made frequent trips to the field to coordinate the different groups' activities. The commanding general of III MAF, Lt. Gen. Robert E. Cushman, Jr., did not approve of my request to move my headquarters into the field since, as an assistant chief of staff, I could better coordinate the activities with the communications we had available in Da Nang. The Combined Action Program was coordinated at the level of General Cushman and Lt. Gen. Hoang Xuan Lam, the Vietnamese Commander of I Corps.

I did go on operations with the CAGs whenever possible. I also selected different patrols, but for security reasons I never indicated which one. I didn't want any undue preparation by the patrol just because I would be accompanying it. When the patrol departed, they put out OPs at key points that acted as a rearguard security and caught up to the main body later on. We would stop at the home of a village elder and, over a cup of tea, he and I would discuss how the CAP could better protect his hamlet. MEDCAPs were always mentioned, as were building schools and repairing damaged structures. In essence we were attempting to coordinate all the Marine functions in the hamlet through the CAP. I spent quite a bit of time with the different platoons doing this.

Assigning a regular ARVN unit to the CAP, I believe, would not have enhanced operations. We probably would have had considerable competition over authority and jurisdiction. As it was, there was very little question about the command structure within the CAP. It went to the Marines in the field, supported by the PFs.

The political situation in Saigon did not affect us that much. However, I must admit, the political situation did dictate at times to what village a CAP would be assigned. This was due, I imagine, to a personal or family situation.

The Vietnamese thought that the presence of one of our platoons in a very remote or uncontested area would be a waste of manpower. We were not in a position to debate the location of any CAP; our objective was to maintain security and increase the pacification effort.

The Marine Corps provided the CAPs with as much support as possible. We also received excellent medical support, not only from the corpsmen in the field but also from medical personnel of both Marine divisions, since both had CAPs within their TAORs.

We had outstanding support from the 1st Marine Division in the recruitment of personnel, and good support from the 3d Marine Division. When it became necessary to replenish the personnel for the CAPs, each division was given a quota of personnel—we usually needed twenty-five Marines from each division on the first day of the following month to replace Marines who were going back to the United States. I had a tremendous working relationship with Lt. Col. Wally Green of the 1st Marine Division. He provided me with the service record books of those applying for the program, and we scanned them to make certain the individuals had good proficiency and conduct marks, had served in combat, had sufficient time remaining in country, and had no prior offenses. Then, accompanied by another CAG officer, I conducted a personal interview with the Marines and from this we selected between 65 and 70 percent of the candidates.

We did have occasions where first sergeants would submit lists of people who were not volunteers and had no idea what the program was about; they were getting rid of their deadwood. However, once these people were interviewed, this was quickly determined and we sent them back to their units immediately.

Viet Cong and NVA forces were a dedicated opponent, no question about that. Nonetheless, we were a formidable force ourselves. The VC were good at infiltrating. We had an incident in the 4th CAG where a returning patrol thought to be one of ours chewed up one of the CAPs quite mercilessly. Several of the PFs had peeled off and joined up with the VC and led them right to the CAP's position. This infiltration was a constant threat to a CAP.

Of course, there were circumstances that showed another side to being a CAP Marine. One Marine had served his full tour, returned home for thirty days, and come back to his unit. He was killed in a firefight trying to protect his hamlet from a VC attack. I went to that hamlet and saw that the villagers had completely covered his body with flowers, demonstrating their love and respect for this Marine who had given his life in support of their cause.

We also experienced some distrust between Marines and PFs. For example, one Marine accidentally killed a PF returning from a patrol. The Vietnamese soldier had gone out as he should have, but then he'd broken off from the platoon and was returning to the CAP compound earlier than expected. The Marine on watch was not expecting anybody to return that early and mistakenly shot him. Well, the other PFs thought the Marine had killed their fellow soldier intentionally, and it took quite a bit of determination on my part to extract that Marine from that CAP. The PFs wanted to administer their own brand of justice, but I did succeed in getting him out of that village. You might say I was held hostage for a short period when the PFs would not permit my jeep to exit the village, but I was able to reestablish authority and leave the area after everything was under control.

One of the saddest events centered around a Marine I had selected for the program from the 1st Marine Division. He was a handsome black Marine, six foot three inches tall, not an ounce of fat on him, and spoke very well. He had served eight months in country, had just been promoted to corporal, and was dedicated. I was very impressed with him and assigned him to the 1st CAG in Chu Lai. I was told he performed his duties as a squad leader in an outstanding manner. He requested a six-month extension for Vietnam, which I gladly approved. He was allowed thirty days' leave, anywhere in the world. The corporal chose to return to his home in Pittsburgh, Pennsylvania. We received notice a few days later that he had missed his plane and was absent without leave. For twenty days we did not hear from him, and then one day out of the blue, he reappeared at 1st CAG headquarters. He had rejoined his old unit in the 1st Marine Division and gone out on operations with them. This may sound illogical, but knowing him as I did, I accepted that explanation.

However, his reception at 1st CAG in Chu Lai was not warm. A warrant officer barked at him something like, "Wait until the colonel gets a hold of you!" Well, the Marine was so upset he shot

Col. Edward F. Danowitz

and killed the warrant officer. I appeared at his court martial and testified in his behalf. I felt I knew psychologically what had triggered the emotion that had prompted him to commit this terrible act. However despite my efforts he was found guilty and sentenced to fifteen years at Fort Leavenworth. Next to a Marine losing his life in Vietnam while performing his duties, this was one of the most painful experiences I had to contend with.

During a tour of Phuoc Thien, Binh Son, Quang Ngai Province, I had the pleasure to accompany Assistant Commandant of the Marine Corps Gen. Lew Walt. I had served with him and knew him personally. He was glad to get back to Vietnam and be with the CAGs, because when he was the CG of III MAF he was one of the original proponents of the program. He envisioned the CAPs as a mobile force where they could destroy the VC and not be located themselves, and not be stuck behind some sandbagged castles in the middle of nowhere.

When we returned to Phuoc Thien, General Walt was warmly remembered by the village elders, who presented him with a unique gift—a hollow drum constructed from a tree about two and a half feet in length and eight inches in diameter. The drum was a warning device for the CAP, PFs, and the villagers. It was placed on the outermost fringes of the village, with a sentinel beating on it all night. The beating of the drum was not to signal the presence of an aggressor force, but to indicate that all was clear. If it stopped, something was wrong.

Vietnam was an impoverished country where you had a population depleted of its strength through mobilization. The country was fighting for its survival, and you couldn't help but support it because of the genuine desire the hamlets and villages had for that survival. Not necessarily for the survival of the political factions in Saigon—that was too far away. But for their own survival.

I would say that the longer the CAPs were there, the greater the cooperation between the Marines and the Vietnamese. We were not there as liberators, but as protectors and coordinators in a combined program. That was the key. Our objective was not to run the hamlet or the village, but to align ourselves with the PFs and the administrative heads to safeguard the area. I felt that the longer the Marines stayed, the better off the villagers were.

★   ★   ★

In September 1969, upon completion of his tour in Vietnam, Colonel Danowitz returned to Quantico, Virginia, and served as Assistant Director, Marine Corps Command and Staff College. Retiring from active duty in 1971, he became a professor of Russian and chairman of the Foreign Language Department at Rollins College in Winter Park, Florida. He traveled to the Soviet Union nine times conducting study programs and lecturing. He holds a Ph.D. from the University of Pennsylvania, Philadelphia. Colonel Danowitz retired from Rollins in 1983 and now resides in Altamonte Springs, Florida.

A. W. Sundberg

2d CAG
1969–1970

A. W. "Sunny" Sundberg spent his first tour in Vietnam with Company F, 2d Battalion, 7th Marines. He was sent to CAPs 2-9-2, 2-4-3, and 2-8-3 during his second tour of duty. He was a rifleman and squad leader.

My first Kit Carson scout's name was Chi; he was in his mid-twenties, an NVA mortarman. We met under very unusual circumstances.

On September 2, 1967, I was on my first tour in Vietnam. I was with Fox Company, 2d Battalion, 7th Marines, when our company compound was hit by a mortar barrage. I was wounded by the first shell and Chi was the enemy soldier on the other end of that mortar tube. He also was wounded, when our company lobbed mortars on his position. I found all this out later, when I was on my second tour in a CAP and met Chi. So I became good friends with the man who was my enemy and caused my first wounds in the war. I learned to respect him, and trust him with my life.

The Vietnamese people were very courteous toward us, and some shared their food with us. When they did we always added ours to the pot. I once stored food with a family for two weeks and they didn't touch it. After that we always left supplies with them, and it was always as we left it. The whole family would have been killed if the VC had found out.

I served in 2d CAG in Quang Nam Province, and our villages were Cho Mai, Ap Quan Nam 1, and Ap Quan Nam 2. The houses were built out of straw, or sometimes artillery cases with tin roofs, which we provided. Most had dirt floors, but a few had wood or concrete. The people cooked their meals over an open pit. Most had their own rice paddies they worked in, and some farmed jointly. A water buffalo cost a year's wages. That was their tractor. Everyone worked together to harvest the rice, and we helped sometimes. The people were very industrious; they made all their own tools, furniture, and homes. I respected them.

Some of the farmers provided us with intelligence, but most just wanted to get on with their lives. They couldn't care less about the war, although it touched them in some way nearly every day.

The village chiefs I met were decent men, and I was on pretty good terms with them. You got no help from the villagers unless you received the chief's confidence. You knew you were accepted once he invited you to his home. He was the mayor, judge, and jury; people came to him to settle all disputes. I know most of them were corrupt, but some weren't. I knew one of them.

I remember this one village elder who'd have nothing to do with me, but then one day Chi informed me that I'd been invited to his home for a meal. I was well received, and after the meal Chi asked, "Did you like your dinner?" I said yes. Then he told me that was good because I'd just eaten our dog. That was Vietnamese humor.

We were a mobile CAP, which I preferred. We ran at least two patrols a day, and I always went on one of them. We observed enemy movement and set up ambushes. My biggest worry was booby traps. We had so many. We blew an average of five a day. One time our CACO commander, a captain, accompanied our patrol on a sweep, and he was wounded by a booby trap! I had to leave half my CAP to provide security for the medevac chopper.

Then we continued on and had to cross a swollen paddy. We spotted the enemy on a hill 600 or 700 meters away. If we crossed we'd be exposed, and in waist-high water. Nobody wanted to go. Finally I jumped into the paddy and began wading toward the objective. My radio operator followed me. As rounds splashed all around us, he asked for soap. He thought it would be a fine time to take a much-needed bath. We both just laughed and raced across the paddy in fire-team rushes. The PFs saw these crazy Marines charging and decided to join us. We all made it.

Most patrols were hot and boring. Once, though, we got caught in a nice L-shaped ambush the VC set up for us; they were on our left flank and to our front. We lay behind a rice paddy dike until our CACO sent in the reactionary force. We had one PF wounded and we lost one CAP member—our dog, Scout. Scout hated the VC and died attacking their position. He was a true CAP Marine. The enemy finally withdrew and we found blood trails but no bodies.

We were involved in civic action all the time. We got supplies to build a school and we even built a well. Some of the Marines sent for clothing and gave it out to the villagers. Twice a week we held MEDCAPs; my second wound was the result of a MEDCAP. A VC tossed a grenade at the corpsman and me. Others were wounded too, including civilians.

If the PFs were not trained properly it was the CAP leader's fault. As with my Marines, they learned by example and some were good and trainable; others were totally useless. I don't know how they found their way into a CAP.

While I was in the second tour with my CAP in 1970, my father passed away and I had to go home on emergency leave. Before I left I told the corporal who was relieving me not to go into the place we called the Little Orchard, because it was heavily booby-trapped. On my return I found that half my CAP was KIA and WIA because this corporal disregarded my advice and took the platoon into the Little Orchard.

I witnessed some heroic deeds by CAP Marines; one black Marine stands out in my mind. I think this was CAP 2-9-2. His first act of bravery was on a patrol. As we moved over this knoll someone screamed, "Booby trap!" Everybody immediately froze. One of our PFs had stepped on a mine that would have exploded if he lifted his foot. This black lance corporal runs straight at the PF, picks him up, and saves him. Luckily no one was hurt. The Marine performed a brave but foolish act.

About three weeks later some Vietnamese kids had entered the old CAP compound and detonated a mine, killing one and wounding two. Again this lance corporal sprang into action and dashed right into the mine field, bringing out the two wounded children.

I should've written him up for a decoration both times, but I didn't know the procedure for writing up someone for a medal. I did report the incidents but forgot about them. That bothers me today. That black Marine should have been decorated for valor, but now I can't remember his name.

I truly believe that the Combined Action Program was the way to win the Vietnamese to our side; at least our CAP was very successful. Ask the Vietnamese people—the villagers—they know. Of all the things I've done, being a CAP leader was my most rewarding assignment.

★　★　★

Since his discharge from the Marine Corps in 1976, Arnie Sundberg has had numerous jobs. He is currently a fish-buyer on the Columbia River in Oregon.

Rocky Jay

4th CAG
1969

Following in his father's footsteps, Rocky Jay enlisted in the Marine Corps in 1968. He was assigned to 4th CAG upon arrival in Vietnam and served in CAP 4-3-6 until he was seriously wounded on October 5, 1969.

All the 0300s [infantry] in my staging battalion at Camp Pendleton were asked if they'd like to volunteer for CAG duty. A lieutenant gave us a BS line about CAG, like going to the rear for thirty days at a time and two cold beers every day.

We arrived in Vietnam May 1, 1969. I flew in on a civilian airline with two grunts and a Navy corpsman, all three going back for a second tour. As we landed in Da Nang one turned to me and said, "Well boot, where you headed?" I said I had orders to III Marine Amphibious Force to a CAG unit. They all hollered, "CAG unit!" I asked them if they knew anything about them. The corpsman said, "Yeah, we're always going out and picking up what's left of 'em."

We flew on a C-130 to Quang Tri, but we couldn't land because the airstrip was catching rockets, so we flew further north into Dong Ha. There we got on a truck and rode into Quang Tri. Sitting outside one of the hootches near 4th CAG headquarters I could see artillery flashes and explosions in the mountains toward the west, but I was so tired I found a rack and went to sleep.

The next morning six of us were standing tall in front of the colonel, who told us we'd be going to 4th CAG. A corporal took pictures of us shaking the colonel's hand and later we were saying how nice it was that the colonel had taken the time out of his busy schedule to have his picture taken with us. The corporal just laughed and told us they were for body identification if we got blown away.

The next day I went to my ville, between Quang Tri and Dong Ha. Heck, I was in pretty good shape, nineteen years old and 185 pounds. A guy walks toward me wearing a pair of cutoff shorts and a couple of bandoliers of ammunition, carrying an M-16, with sandals on his feet! He looked like he weighed no more than 130 pounds. He said he was from Oklahoma and he was with the CAP. The other guys also weighed maybe 130 pounds. I thought to myself, I got to fight a war with these guys? They look horrible! They couldn't fight their way out of nothing. They sure didn't look like any Marines I ever knew or saw.

After a week I went to CAP school in Da Nang. I got excited when I saw all my buddies from boot camp, ITR, and staging. There must have been 200 of us there. We'd already taken a few casualties, mostly in 1st and 2d CAG. I think we had six killed that first week. It was reality.

I stayed in Da Nang two weeks. School was on the beach in an old French compound, and they had pallets of ice-cold beer for us. We listened to good music on tape players, songs like "In the Ghetto" by Elvis Presley and "In the Year 2525." I guess that's what I remember most.

Every morning the instructors began by reading us the After Action Reports filed by CAP units from the night before. These included enemy KIA and WIA, weapons captured, and Marine KIAs and WIAs. It didn't take us too long to figure out that there wouldn't be many of us around at the end of our tours.

When I went back to Quang Tri they issued me a flak jacket and helmet. But at the 4th CAG headquarters a gunny sergeant said, "Just drop that flak jacket and helmet in that pile over there, Marine. It's not going to do you any good where you're going." What good could a flak jacket do against a company of NVA regulars?

My CAG was 4-3-5, 4th CAG, 3d Company, 5th Platoon. We were just south of the Cua Viet River and north of Quang Tri—pretty far north. We had one of the largest AOs in northern I Corps. The southern boundary of the AO was a dirt path and the northern boundary was the Cua Viet River. It had large sand dunes, like in the movie *Lawrence of Arabia*, swampy areas, and triple-canopy jungle.

There were nine Marines in that unit—a corporal, a couple of lance corporals, and the rest PFCs and privates. Most of them were good ol' Southern boys. We didn't have a corpsman. Seems the CAP had a hard time keeping one.

Our CAP leader was Sgt. Gary Nelson. He was on his second

tour and was a mother hen to us all. Gary was the finest Marine I ever met.

At first I was treated with a cool hand. I hadn't proven myself yet. The old salts all thought CAG was going to hell. Here I was a boot straight from staging, put right into a CAG unit. All the other guys had at least six months in country before being assigned to a CAG. We're gonna get killed keeping this boot alive, they said. But I gained their confidence. Hell, I was the second-oldest one there.

Between the nine of us we had three PRC-25 radios, one M-60 machine gun, three bloopers, a 12-gauge shotgun, one M-14, various claymores [mines], and LAWs [light antitank weapons]. Everyone carried an M-16 with seventeen magazines with seventeen rounds in each magazine. We moved every night.

The new guy always got to carry the radio because it was added weight and you were a prime target for the enemy. I knew nothing about radios. Here I am loaded down with the radio, frags, ammo, claymores, and LAWs. While I was in Vietnam a man landed on the moon. I remember thinking they could put a man on the moon but the Marine Corps couldn't get me a jackass to carry all this gear.

On three or four occasions we had language problems with the PFs. The translation would be lost and somebody would get insulted, and before you knew it there'd be eight Marines on one side and twenty-five or thirty PFs on the other locked and loaded. I'd be in the middle trying to raise the actual [commanding officer] on the radio to ask what the hell to do. They'd recognize my Texas drawl and say, "Here's that old Texas boy in trouble again!"

One day a friend and I decided to head out to the sand dunes. Lizard had just gotten a new M-60 machine gun and wanted to test-fire it. I carried about 100 blooper rounds to fire across the dunes. If I'd been hit carrying all those M-79 rounds I would've gone off like a 105-mm round. Anyway, I'm popping off these blooper rounds when a radio message comes in saying an Army unit just got ambushed in the northern part of our AO. Well, we were *in* the northern part of our AO, so we stopped and listened a bit more, but didn't hear anything. The Army column had reported that they were taking heavy mortar and machine-gun fire. We listened a bit; then Lizard and I looked at each other.

We crawled to the top of one of the sand dunes and, peering

over the top, saw a bunch of APCs in a circle. It looked like a wagon train. We snuck back to our ville and kept quiet. I'm sure Lizard and I were responsible for getting those Army guys their Combat Infantry Badges that day.

I guess the reason the Combined Action Program worked so well, at least in our CAG, was the fact we knew our AO so well. The regular grunt units left and returned six weeks later, but we knew every bush, stick, and bend in the river where an ambush could be set for us.

We had thirty PFs. They were like a National Guard unit— a bunch of draft dodgers. They were always busting ambushes. Another Marine and I would take them out to the sand dunes and leave them out there all night just to get away from them.

I used a unique method to keep our PFs awake on ambush at night. They got salty with you every once in a while and stood up to you so I decided to do something. My parents sent me a big slingshot from home. I'd take the 00-buck out of a shotgun round and use them for ammunition. If I caught a PF sleeping I'd knock him over with it. He wouldn't know what hit 'im. It'd raise a knot on his head or back the size of a handball. After a while, they kept their eyes open.

We had two Kit Carson scouts; one had been in a VC unit before joining us. He was so totally useless, we used to say the VC kicked him out. We heard he was caught selling medical supplies on the black market and was eliminated.

The other Kit Carson had been with a hardcore NVA unit, and he was good! He hated the PFs and had nothing to do with them. He was about six feet, tall for a Vietnamese, and always wore a red T-shirt. He spoke pretty good English. He told me he'd Chieu Hoi'd to the U.S. Army because he was afraid to give himself up to the Marines. But after that he joined the Marines because he liked us, I guess. He said when the Marines left he'd leave; he knew the South Vietnamese Army couldn't operate by themselves. He was a good guy. I always wondered what happened to him.

After three months I was second in seniority. Everyone else had either been hit or rotated. We set up ambushes, usually made up of two or three Marines and six PFs. We had total control over our villages. We tried to stop any infiltration and had specific rules set up with the village chief. We told him explicitly that if anyone stepped out at night they were game. We ruled the roost in the hours of darkness. That's the way it had to be, because nighttime was always Charlie's time to operate and we were trying to take it away from him. You didn't have time to ask questions; you just opened up and checked later on. We had a sixth sense, probably because we were country boys, old squirrel hunters. Nobody ventured in our AO. I really believe the thing that kept me alive was my tremendous night vision and hearing. As long as someone was watching my rear I knew I'd be okay. I could hear 'em and smell 'em long before I could see 'em. I guess it was a gift.

We wouldn't tell anybody the location of our ambush sites, and we had code names for places. Grand Central Junction was the crossroads near the river. Even our PFs didn't know what these names meant, because there could have been a VC agent among them. Who knew?

After two months I needed a break and went back to Quang Tri to get some medication for my feet. My clothes were rotting off and I weighed 139 pounds. I guess I was a true CAG Marine.

It was a different type of warfare. Sometimes we'd be just forty feet from the enemy and let loose with LAWs and grenades. Tracers would be going off in every direction. Sometimes it lasted thirty seconds, but it was fierce. It always amazed me that in such a small area, with so many people, sometimes no one would get hurt. Other times one frag would explode and three or four people would get wounded.

Our combat was night after night. You just did it until you were killed, wounded, or rotated. I was amazed at the guys that had been there since '67 or '68. They were independent and had a seabag full of Purple Hearts, but they didn't want to go home. They loved being the hunter. In a grunt unit you were one of a large mass of ants looking for Mr. Charles, and most of the time he found you. It was different with us.

I heard that in 1971, when they were deactivating the CAGs, a couple of the guys stayed behind in the villes. If that's true, I'd like to know what happened to them. True individualists. A little crazy maybe, but individualists just the same.

I guess we must've done a good job because the gooks put a price on our heads. One CAP unit killed a VC one time and discovered our names and medevac numbers written on a piece of paper. I remember writing my parents that I finally made something out of my life; I was worth something.

The villagers were so tired of the war they really didn't care who controlled things. They just wanted to be left alone. Some of them shared their hootches, their food, their laughter, and their tears with us.

One thing I learned real fast was to stay friendly with the kids. As long as kids were around I felt comfortable, but if no kids or PFs showed up I knew I was in for a long, uneasy night. Our sister CAP just south of us killed a VC who turned out to be the daddy of one of our ville's kids. That was part of life in Vietnam.

I read that out of the 5,000 Marines in CAG, we took 30 percent fatalities, had an 80 to 85 percent chance of getting wounded once and a 50 percent chance of getting wounded twice. Despite this, many Marines extended their tours in CAP.

We had good support until September 1969, when the Marines started pulling out and they put the Army in there. The Army really didn't understand what we were trying to accomplish in CAG. They came out in their APCs, loaded with cases of beer and soda, wearing flak jackets and helmets. There we were in cut-offs with no protection. They couldn't understand these stupid Marines living in villages with the gooks. I felt like Lawrence of Arabia riding around on those APCs. Well, about nightfall they'd leave. They didn't like staying with us in the ville at night.

My luck ran out on October 5, 1969. You might say five is my unlucky number: I was wounded five months after landing in Vietnam, five days after getting promoted to lance corporal, five days after being assigned to another CAP unit, at five o'clock in the morning. I was hit five times, they got five out of seven of us, and I spent five months in the hospital. It took me a year to learn how to walk again.

One thing that sticks in my mind about that day: As I lay there bleeding in the mud with the rain hitting me in the face, one of the PFs was crawling around on his hands and knees. He saw me and crawled over to me. I saw that he'd suffered a horrible head wound. He wiped my face and lay down next to me. I don't even remember the guy's name. I should know his name.

After I got back I wrote to get my records. They told me they never heard of CAP. At our first reunion some colonel spoke, saying that two-thirds of the people in the CAP wouldn't qualify to enter the Marine Corps today. Some of those boys didn't have high-school diplomas. But we were good. We were damn good.

Here it is over twenty years later and two of my neighbors are Vietnamese. I guess things really have come full circle.

★　　★　　★

Rocky Jay is married and co-owner of a medical-supply company in Abilene, Texas. He is one of the founders of the Abilene Grunts' Association. Every February the group holds its Tet party. He is still an avid hunter.

John A. Daube

2d CAG
1969

After enlisting in the U.S. Navy, John A. Daube was trained as a medical corpsman and sent to Vietnam. He was assigned to a CAP in the An Hoa area, a hotbed of enemy activity in 1969. He stayed in the CAPs until he was wounded and medevaced to Japan and, eventually, the United States.

The first target of choice was the CAP leader, the second the radio operator, and the third the hospital corpsman. I was a hospital corpsman.

Our CAP was located near An Hoa, home of the 5th Marines. We stayed in the bush and only came to the rear when we absolutely had to. The area was hot. The villages were anywhere from one to a half a click apart. We stayed on the move constantly. At night, when we could, we slept in the cemeteries. The Vietnamese believed that to enter a cemetery of their loved ones was bad. We also slept near dung piles out in the middle of rice paddies. The Vietnamese stayed away from there for obvious reasons. Our CAP always slept in full combat gear, rifles across our laps, propped up against gravestones, trees, rocks, whatever.

I carried an M-16, .45-caliber pistol, M-79 grenade launcher at times, Willie Peter, and frags. Our CAP had two M-60 machine guns, two BARs, and an infrared scope. We were heavily armed.

We usually split into two groups at night and established perimeters around the various hamlets to protect the villagers from assassination. During the day we linked up with patrols from the 5th Marines or just basically hid out and slept.

The terrain surrounding the An Hoa area was rough. It was nearly impossible to get vehicles in and out, so we walked everywhere. There was this one wagon trail that the villagers used to get to the big marketplace at An Hoa. A jeep could travel on it, but it was real tough on its suspension system. We did transport several wounded Marines, but they were in such pain that we felt in the future it would be more humane to call in a medevac chopper.

The villagers tolerated us because they realized we were trying to save their country from falling to communism, but they didn't like the fact that we kept trying to Americanize them. There were certain things we did that they could just not understand, like carrying a cloth around in our pocket, blowing our nose into it, and then putting it back in our pocket. They wiped their noses on a banana leaf or just blew it on the ground. If they had to go to the bathroom, they went to a community pile and defecated near the bottom of it. Certain individuals in the village were designated to take the fresh feces and place it on the top of the heap. It was a huge human compost pile, and they used it to fertilize their crops. It was quite effective, because they had tremendous rice and peanut plants in the area.

The kids were fascinated by us. By hanging around they knew they could get candy and cigarettes. They just loved us, or so we thought. In actuality they were using us.

One day a Vietnamese boy about eight years old approached our group wearing a knapsack. It looked like the bookbags kids use today. It was in the middle of the summer, so we were pretty certain there was no school. A reflection of the sun highlighted a wire that ran over the kid's shoulder and down his arm. One of the Marines shot him. As the child fell, he pulled the wire and blew himself up. This may sound barbaric to some, but it was common for the VC to sacrifice their children just to kill a few Marines.

The river that ran through our AO was very, very brown and obviously polluted. The Vietnamese bathed in it and never removed the bottom half of their clothing. While they washed, water buffalo dung floated by, or an occasional dead body— ARVN, NVA, VC. The Vietnamese could not fathom why we washed in one of the village wells. To us it was clear water, cool and refreshing, but to them it was a waste of good drinking water.

In the middle of the summer the villagers invited us to a big feast, some sort of national holiday. It was not Tet because it was summertime. I remember the temperature reaching around 120 degrees that day. They had foot races and we introduced them to a tug-of-war. They roasted a couple of pigs in the village square, and at the banquet we discovered through Hippie, a French-speaking Marine in our CAP, that we were also eating fried pig's brains and fish entrails.

Our AO was heavily infiltrated by NVA and VC forces and we

John A. Daube

made contact two to three times a week. One night our CAP established a perimeter in the backyard of this house. I sat down and quickly dozed off. Suddenly I woke up to a PF whispering at me, "Bac-Si! Bac-Si! VC! VC!" I reached down and put my glasses on to see the advance party of an NVA battalion about twenty yards away from me. Miraculously, they didn't see us. We quickly formed a tighter perimeter and opened fire on them. We had another group near us who ran over and soon we had them in a crossfire. But there were only fourteen of us and we were easily overrun. We regrouped and, luckily for us, they skirted our CAP and continued on to An Hoa, where there was a Marine base. We alerted the Marines and saw one hell of a firefight from our position overlooking the combat base. The ammo dump exploded and we watched in amazement as the shock waves rippled toward us. When it hit, the concussion of the blast knocked two Marines unconscious and everyone got nose bleeds and ringing in the ears.

Two from our CAP were killed that night, a Marine and a PF. The PF sergeant didn't understand why I couldn't save his man's life, but he had a massive head injury and his brains were literally hanging out. It was very difficult for me to communicate to the Vietnamese sergeant that there was nothing I could do for this wounded PF. I wrapped his head in a battle dressing and made him as comfortable as I could. We couldn't get any choppers out to us right away. There was nothing I could do for him. Nothing.

On another patrol I was taking up the rear. We were about twelve yards apart from each other. Well . . . my night vision isn't very good, never has been, and to complicate matters we had a quarter moon that night. Suddenly I found myself in this mud pit, buried up to my chest. At first I thought it was quicksand and I was a goner for sure, but I only sank up to my chest. I couldn't get out, and I couldn't get my rifle off my shoulder. I was terrified. I felt for sure an enemy patrol would find me and blow me away. I didn't want to holler out for fear of alerting enemy troops in the area, so the rest of the patrol just kept going. It seemed like hours had passed, but I think it was only fifteen minutes before the patrol doubled back to find me. God . . . I'll never forget that night.

My very first patrol I got in a firefight. I remember a Marine by the name of Private First Class Rowan yelling to me, "Fire at their tracers, Doc!" That was okay, but we had tracers too, which meant they could do the same to us. Nobody was hit, but a couple of their people were hit. I heard them screaming. And we found blood trails. That was my first taste of combat. When it was finished, my pants were wet and soiled. But it felt good to flip an M-16 on full automatic and let it rip. It was a feeling of power and fear at the same time.

I also provided medical care. I treated everything—boils, bunions, rashes included. The more serious cases I sent to An Hoa. The Seabees had erected a pretty good-size school at Phu Du Mot, but unfortunately it sat idle, so I used it for my sick bay. That was the extent of our CAP's civic-action efforts. We were too busy trying to keep from getting killed.

I think the CAPs were successful as far as the combat aspect was concerned—we captured arms and food caches and we had a lot of confirmed kills. But medically, I think it was a failure. I bet you I could travel back to Vietnam today, to those same villages, and still find them beating their clothes on rocks and bathing in that filthy river.

I was a hospital corpsman and trained to save lives, but I did kill a few of the enemy while I was in Vietnam. That didn't bother me while I was there, but after I returned home I thought about it a lot.

★   ★   ★

John Daube lives in Trumansburg, New York, with his family. He is a registered professional nurse and an advanced emergency medical technician. He works for the fire department and for a professional ambulance service. He is also an enthusiastic member of Chapter 377 of the Vietnam Veterans of America.

Jack Broz

1st CAG
1969

Arriving in Vietnam, U.S. Navy corpsman Jack Broz was assigned to Company A, 1st Battalion, 4th Marines. When that unit left Vietnam he was reassigned to 1-4-1, south of Chu Lai, the southernmost CAP in South Vietnam.

In August 1969 we got word that the 3d Marine Division was leaving Vietnam. We jumped for joy. Then we found out that the pullout was on paper only. Those of us with 100 days or less left in country were to be reassigned to other units.

CAP 1-4-1 was the southernmost Marine unit in all of Vietnam. On clear nights we could see the lights at Quang Ngai, the biggest city to the south of us. Our AO ran along Highway 1. We were due east of My Lai 1, My Lai 2, My Lai 3, and My Lai 4, but they weren't in our AO. Other villages I recall were Khanh Van 4 and Khanh Van 5, Phu Ninh, Dong Thanh 1, Phong Nien, and Duyen Phuoc. It was pretty countryside, with lots of rice paddies surrounding the hamlets. It was also flat, which was a change for me, having spent most of my tour in the mountains up north.

Khanh Van 4 was a strange place. There was a huge building where we normally made our day pos. It looked like it might have been a French plantation once.

I was the old man in CAP 1-4-1, at age twenty. Out of all the Americans in the unit, I'd seen the most combat. The other guys thought I never got scared. Little did they know I was doing everything in my power not to be.

At first I felt strange walking into the villages. I wasn't used to it. There were ten of us and twenty or thirty PFs. We called them the Quans, short for Nghia Quans. They ranged in age from eighteen to sixty, mostly farmers who lived nearby. There was one who never did any work—my counterpart, a Vietnamese medic. He just hung around his house.

The PF chain of command was Trung-si Nhat, Trung-si, and

Ha-si Nhat. The Trung-si Nhat translated into staff sergeant. He was a lot older and wasn't around much. They said he'd fought against the Japanese and the French. Whether he was VC or not, I couldn't say.

Then there was Trung-si, or the sergeant. He was a shithead. Just worthless. If the brass wasn't around, he wasn't around. He was constantly raiding my medical kit and stealing medicine, especially if he thought there was something of value. He always volunteered to carry the box when we changed locations.

One day I made a big to-do about administering every Marine a tablet wrapped in shiny colored paper. I made sure he saw me give it to them. None of the Marines, of course, took it; it was Ex-lax. Sure enough, that night all my Ex-lax tablets disappeared. The next day the Vietnamese medic came up to me and could hardly contain himself he was laughing so hard. He said, "All night long, Trung-si, beaucoup shit!"

Trung-si never stole from my medical kit again.

The Ha-si Nhat, or corporal, was pretty much the one in charge. He wore a new uniform every day, complete with an orange silk scarf and sunglasses. I never saw him without his sunglasses on. He was very aggressive and led our PF contingent quite well. Too well, as far as the Vietnamese were concerned.

Just before I rotated there was a loud explosion one night. At first we thought the VC had entered the wire and mortared us. But, as we later found out, the Ha-si Nhat was out setting up claymores, and as he was walking back toward the perimeter one went off. He was hit by the backblast. When they asked the PFs who was near the detonators, they said a cow stepped on it. Now, anyone who has detonated a claymore knows it'd be pretty difficult for a cow to set one off. We felt certain he was fragged by his own troops. He was hit in the lower legs and back by the pellets. The next morning we found his jungle boot; it'd been blown off in the blast and had burned from the lower heel to the eyelets. That's how powerful the blast was. It was too risky to send for a medevac chopper that late, so I kept him medicated all night. At dawn the medevac chopper flew in and I carried him to the helicopter. I never saw him again.

There was one ville we only traveled to at night; its name escapes me now. It was on the east side of Highway 1. We always heard the sound of drums in the distance when we went there. Rhythmic drumming. The villagers told us it was a way to warn us if the VC were on the move.

Jack Broz

I had a conversation with one of the Vietnamese from that village one evening. He had had a little too much to drink and was chattering away. He said to me, "Go home. Go home." I said we were there to help them. Then he said, "Long time got VC. Few people die. Americans come, got many VC, many people die." I'll never forget that night and what he said.

The Vietnamese person I recall the most vividly was a young crippled kid; couldn't have been more than twelve years old. He told me he liked Marines because they had saved his life years ago when he was struck by a mortar shell. There were big chunks of flesh missing from his legs and he walked with a limp. He followed us around like a puppy and wore a battered old Marine utility cap.

We had nicknames for everything. There was a small clump of villages in our AO we called Tits, because one of its inhabitants was a rather overly endowed woman. Almost all Vietnamese women are small, slender, and small-breasted. But not Tits. She was pretty, too. And when she smiled you could see two gold teeth on either side of her mouth. It looked like a car's headlights. Needless to say, all the guys wanted to get to know Tits, but she kept her distance.

Whenever we could, which was about every other day, we washed our clothes and ourselves. We also had what we called a bathe-in, which attracted a group of children. The older kids pushed the little ones toward us and asked us to wash them. We poured buckets of water over them, soaping them up and rinsing them off. We had a good time and so did the kids. For some of them, it was probably the only bath they got.

I had to radio in a weekly report of the number of civilians I treated. And I did keep records. I was short [near the end of one's tour of duty] and wanted back to the rear. Sometimes I doctored the numbers and made them smaller than they should have been; I figured if they thought I wasn't treating that many villagers they'd pull me out and send me to the rear. It didn't work that way, though. As I was getting ready to rotate I asked the Chief why, with my low numbers, I wasn't pulled out of the field. He said mine were the only numbers they believed!

I treated quite a few babies in my MEDCAPs. Oddly enough, most of the time the young children carried the infants to me, not the parents. Most of these babies had their heads covered with running sores. I treated the babies with a technique I learned up north for jungle rot. I took some Furacin ointment and smeared it liberally all over the baby's head, with a tongue blade. Then I wrapped my own special bandage that I devised around its head, complete with chin strap. I told the kid to bring the baby back in a couple of days so I could change the dressing. Most never came back, but one youngster did return with a baby to show me that the sores had healed.

I got a taste of medicine Vietnamese-style at Tits's place one day. One of our PFs was running a fever and I was trying to treat him. One of the elder Vietnamese, known as Pop, told me the villagers would tend to him. "You give medicine to Americans," he said.

I got to watch what they did. Two older men entered the room, each carrying glass containers. They looked like those small toilet-water bottles I'd seen girls carry back home, and they had a bluish-green liquid in them. They had the PF take off his shirt. Then they put a broken water glass over a flame, and when they figured it was hot enough they cut a series of little pricks up and down his spine and on each temple, using the glass. Then the Vietnamese elders placed a drop of this liquid on their fingers and rubbed it into each cut. Next—and I swear this is true—they took a bird's nest, a spider's web, and a wasp's nest, and placed them in boiling water. After mixing this concoction to their satisfaction, they made the poor PF drink it! When he finished they laid him back down and placed a bucket of hot coals under his bed. A short time later he vomited. He was no better by morning, so I called for a medevac for treatment in the rear. About a week later he rejoined our CAP.

Every evening we'd pack up and be on the move to establish new positions. From there we'd send out ambushes; one or two a night. Theoretically, this was to keep the VC from knowing where we were, which in our case was a bunch of garbage. They knew where we were all the time. It was impossible to keep it from them. CAP 1-4-1 had been in this area for years, as far as I could tell, and everybody knew us.

Most times we didn't follow procedure, and occasionally we

wouldn't even send out the ambushes. Back at 1st CAG headquarters at Chu Lai, they monitored the CAP ambushes all night. However, we weren't where we said we were. What we did was set up a huge ambush around the ville we were in. We realized we couldn't repulse a large enemy attack, and by keeping ourselves in a tight group we felt we had a better chance if we were assaulted.

We got one hot meal a day, weather permitting of course. It was flown into us by the Americal Division, who were all around us. We were in an area that couldn't be resupplied easily by truck. A Huey dropped off metal containers of hot food plus three or four cartons of C-rats. We always shared our food with the PFs and the people of whatever ville we were in.

This one time, because of a bad fog, the chopper couldn't get in with our supplies. We ran out of C-rats. The PFs went into Quang Ngai and brought us packages of dried noodles, and they went out in the fields and brought in a vegetable that looked like a sweet potato but was white. They roasted them and gave them to us. We also boiled some water and cooked the noodles. What was amazing about this was the PFs paid for the noodles themselves. Incredible, since the average PF, in our CAP anyway, earned the equivalent of ten dollars a month, or less. I'll never forget what the PFs did for us that day.

Interacting with the Vietnamese had its moments. One evening the Vietnamese medic came up to me with a concerned look on his face. I asked what was the matter.

"I have heard on the radio and read stories that say Americans have gone to the moon," he said.

"This is true," I answered.

He beamed and asked, "When you go back to America, will you be able to go to the moon?"

I said no, only majors and colonels could go, and I was just a sergeant.

"Ah," he replied, "it's the same in my army. The officers have all the fun."

Monty was the corporal in charge. His real name was Lamont R. Tillot III. He was a comedian and an excellent Marine. He always laughed and joked with the Vietnamese—and he got things done. He made these elaborate gestures with his hands and got everyone hysterical. It made our relationship with the Vietnamese so much better. Once Monty and I were invited to a feast given at the home of a Vietnamese elder. They'd taught us at CAP school always to leave something on your plate in a Vietnamese home. That means your host prepared enough food and your hunger has been satisfied. If you finish everything, the Vietnamese lose face.

So Monty and I sat down to eat. This was my introduction to Vietnamese cooking and table manners. They put a large rice bowl in front of us, and alongside it other smaller bowls. They put food in the little bowls and watched as we ate it. One of the items placed in my bowl was what looked like a French-fried frog—minus the legs. I just picked it up with my chopsticks and swallowed the thing whole. I didn't even ask what it was. I'd seen them eat it so I thought if it didn't kill them, it wouldn't kill me either.

Next they poured this clear, colorless liquid in my glass and I downed it. My lips, tongue, mouth, and throat felt like they were on fire. Everybody burst out laughing; my eyes must have bugged out of my head. Before I had a chance to say no thank you, they poured more. This time I nursed it.

Then came the big shock. After I finished the drink, one of the Vietnamese poured the contents of his cigarette lighter into my glass! To this day I'm not sure what I drank at that dinner.

Our CAP went on one major operation while I was there. There were a number of small villes that were suspected of being VC, and we had a raid on the village of Dai Loc, situated on the other side of the railroad tracks that ran through our AO. I did not want to go on this raid; I was too short.

That night it started raining, which made it worse. Trying to walk a rice paddy dike in the daytime was bad enough, but at night it's even worse, with the mud. I dressed very carefully. I put my rain gear over my flak jacket and did not wear my helmet. You couldn't hear at night with a helmet on.

We took a circuitous route to Dai Loc so we wouldn't be detected. It seemed like forever to get there. When we arrived and took up our positions, we began moving in on the ville. One of the PFs knocked on the door of one hootch just outside the ville. Whatever was said from inside did not please him one bit, so he kicked the door in and dragged out a couple of people. One was an old papa-san who was yelling at the PF. For his protests, he was kicked in the groin, clubbed by rifle butts, and tied up. A young woman who protested was treated in the same manner, and the Marines just watched. We were told to let the Vietnamese handle this themselves, but I did not approve of the Vietnamese tactics at all.

Then somebody hollered that somebody was running away.

Our PFs started firing and the next thing I know everybody's firing. A flare goes up lighting the night sky. Then we do this John Wayne charge toward the center of the village. I stopped in my tracks just as bullets stitched a path in front of me, and I turned to see this crazy American firing his M-60 in all directions. Everything was happening so fast.

I saw one Vietnamese man run from a house. The PFs ordered him to stop, but he kept going. They fired at him and missed. Then a woman came out of another hut but she was cut down by machine-gun fire. Then I saw the PF corporal fire a LAW at a hootch and I watched as it exploded. A woman stumbled from the burning hootch dragging her children behind her. Her lower jaw was missing.

Soon the entire ville was on fire. We rounded up about twenty people we suspected of being VC sympathizers and marched them toward our AO to be transported to the rear for interrogation. There was one Vietnamese girl that the PFs had singled out. They were really mad at her. I asked why, and they said she'd been married to one of the PFs but had left him for a VC. Now she was making babies for them. We wanted her to make an escape attempt. We would have fired one shot in the air, one at her feet, and then one in the middle of her back. I guess you had to be there to understand it. I think that was the closest I came to really hating while I was there. And yet there was no reason to hate.

Later I heard there were a number of VC in the group we captured; one old man was the VC district chief. But I remember thinking, If the rest of them weren't VC before, they probably are now.

Did we do any good? That's a hard question to answer.

★   ★   ★

Jack Broz participated in the first delayed-stress studies conducted by Dr. John Wilson at Cleveland State University. In 1978, he founded the first Vietnam Vets support group in his county. President Jimmy Carter awarded him the Outstanding Vietnam Era Veteran Award for community service in 1979. Broz lives in Lorain, Ohio, with his wife, Anna, and their three children.

Dr. Wayne Christiansen

2d CAG
1969–1970

Wanting to be a part of the Vietnam experience, Wayne Christiansen enlisted in the U.S. Navy. Upon arrival in South Vietnam in November 1969, he was sent to a CAP in 2d CAG near Hoi An, where he was the platoon corpsman.

When I finally landed at Da Nang Air Base in Vietnam in November 1969, the thing that struck me first was the heat. It was extremely hot and humid. It hit you right away. And there was a strange odor in the air. Jets were flying everywhere and there was barbed wire all over the place. People were scurrying about on foot and in jeeps. It was all very confusing.

After I was processed, someone called out my name and motioned for a bunch of us to jump into the back of a six-by truck. One of the Marines said, "Well guys, you are now in the CAP." I overheard several Marines, who I knew were on their second tour in 'Nam, let out a moan. One of them said, "Oh shit! I don't wanna be a fuckin' hero. I ain't going to no CAP outfit."

My heart sank. What had I gotten myself into?

While we were in CAP school, the corpsmen were sent out on MEDCAPs to the local neighborhoods in Da Nang. These MED-CAPs were run by a Vietnamese nurse we called Sam. We went out with her in groups of three and four to observe. All she did was pass out pills to people. If they said they had a headache, she gave them aspirin. If they said they had stomach problems, she administered charcoal and mint. This went on and on for hours with people pushing and shoving each other. It was unbelievable. I had no idea what she was doing—and neither did she. It was a good example of what not to do in our own villages.

After CAP school graduation we hopped on a jeep to be transported to our CAP. The driver went like a bat out of hell and those of us in the back sat on sandbags in case we hit a land mine. I guess they figured the sandbags would shield us a little from the blast.

My CAP was located in the refugee village of Dai Loc, about thirty miles southwest of Da Nang. Our CACO headquarters was on a hill that we shared with an Army intelligence outfit.

I went into a small room that had been assigned to the corpsmen and stayed up all night reviewing the myriad medications we had in stock. I didn't know which ones I'd need, and I had no idea what three-quarters of them were for. I had a Merck Manual [medical handbook] that I intended to consult when I treated the Marines and civilians.

The next morning I met my actual, a corporal by the name of Patrick Romo. He was a Chicano from Los Angeles. Pat was a very capable individual, real street smart. He was a good Marine and I trusted him immediately, but I'm not so sure he trusted me right away. On our way to my CAP from headquarters, he stopped to turn my helmet around. I had it on backward! It really embarrassed the hell out of me.

Most of the PFs we had in our CAP were shitbirds. There were maybe three or four of them that were decent individuals and really did give a damn about what was going on, but most of them were either too young or too old. You really had to watch them all the time because they would steal from you. Things like transistor radios, clothing, packages from home.

Our PFs all carried M-16s. Some had bandoliers of ammo, some carried rounds in their pockets. A few wore the green canvas-sided jungle boots, the standard issue to all Marines. Most wore sneakers or tennis shoes, high-top black sneakers. On the side of them was written PF Flyers. How appropriate! We started calling them PF Flyers because when things got tough, they flew the coop.

Our Trung-si was a real squared-away guy. His troops really respected him. He would kick the shit out of any of them if they were disrespectful to him. He didn't do it because he was a bully; I guess he thought that was the only method he had to keep them in line.

For about a month I was loaned out to another CAP in our company. Their PFs were downright hostile, sullen, and mean. On night patrol we had to carry metal cans filled with M-60 machine gun ammo. These ammo cans were heavy and we split them up between the Marines and PFs to share the load. I usually

Dr. Wayne Christiansen

carried one myself, sometimes two, even though I was a corpsman. One night before we went out, the PFs decided they weren't going to hump these ammo cans. One of them got in a shoving match with one of the Marines and before we realized it, we were completely surrounded by PFs. There were about twenty of them and twelve of us. Things started to escalate very quickly as everyone locked and loaded. Everything seemed to move in slow motion as the Marines got into crouching positions. I thought to myself, Oh my God, here we go. The shootout at the OK Corral.

Just then the CAP leader and the Trung-si stepped outside. The CAP leader screamed at the top of his voice, "What the fuck is going on here?" Everyone started talking at once. The Trung-si went up to the instigating PF who'd refused to carry the ammo can and kicked him right in the ass. He pointed at the ammo cans and one by one, the Vietnamese picked them up.

Virtually every firefight we were in, four or five of the PFs would fight with us while the rest either ran away or hid. One night, the night we were overrun, we got our butts whipped. Only two PFs stayed. One ended up being disemboweled, but he did make it. I carried him to the medevac chopper with his guts draped all over me. The other got a serious leg wound and was made a permanent cripple.

My Vietnamese counterpart in the CAP, a PF corpsman who was easily fifteen years my senior, wasn't a bad guy, but I did have a problem with him. He asked me one day to get him some penicillin and other medication when I went to the rear, so when I went to CACO headquarters I got him some items. Several days later I asked him what he'd done with the medical supplies I'd brought him. He couldn't find them and had no good explanation to offer as to how they were used. Of course, I discovered what had happened: he'd sold the drugs on the black market. They'd probably ended up in the hands of the VC. I immediately stopped getting him any further supplies, except battle dressings, and he quit bugging me. I went my way and he went his.

Some villagers were outright hostile to us. No young woman, for example, would have anything to do with us. Talking to a Marine was not looked upon with great favor.

I held MEDCAPs almost every day. I remember one incident when an eleven- or twelve-year-old boy was brought to me holding a bloody rag to his left forearm. He had cut himself severely with one of those hook knives the Vietnamese farmers use in harvesting. The boy needed stitches and I'd never sewed anyone up before. I got out my equipment which, by the way, was not sterile. I injected the area with Novocaine and sewed up the wound. This kid did not even whimper. The Vietnamese are a very stoic people. Fortunately, no infection set in and it healed fine. About three weeks later this same boy was arrested for making booby traps for the VC.

Dr. Wayne
Christiansen

133

There was another young fellow who'd had his leg crushed by a half-track several years earlier. I made four or five frustrating trips back to Da Nang and was finally able to secure him a wooden leg. Then he refused to wear it. Nonetheless, just being able to get that wooden leg was immensely gratifying for me.

There was one thing we did in our CAP that the villagers hated. Most often we moved in with them for the day. At daybreak we knocked on the doors of their hootches and they grudgingly opened up and allowed us to enter. This bothered me; it reminded me of our own American history when the Hessian troops were being quartered in Boston during the Revolutionary War. Here we were doing the same thing in Vietnam, only we were the Hessian troops.

I think the people of our village thought the Saigon government was corrupt and not representative of the people. They did not support the South Vietnamese government. I also believe that their motivation for siding with us was fear of reprisals from the enemy.

Our CAP did a good job. If something looked strange, we investigated it. We constantly watched the people and how they reacted. In the evening, the women traveled down the road to Dai Loc to stay with family and friends for the night. If there was a larger number than usual making the trip, we knew something was up.

By 1970 Vietnamization was in full swing, but with Vietnamization, our artillery, mortars, and reaction forces were disappearing month by month. And we had to rely more and more on the ARVN for support. We were reluctant to call in artillery strikes because you didn't know where the hell the shells were going to land. When you radioed in grid coordinates you had to go through an interpreter; it took forever. Also, we were always low on ammunition and C-rations, so as 1970 rolled on, we felt our CAP was becoming an even more dangerous place to be.

The enemy picked up on this, of course. The NVA and VC became increasingly bold in their attacks, at a time when everyone back home thought things were slowing down. They even started taking us on in broad daylight. Stuck out in the sticks, without adequate support, my CAP started to feel abandoned.

Our CACO commander drank heavily. He came out on ambush with us only two or three times in the nine months I was with the CAP, and he smelled of alcohol. After half an hour or so, he'd pass out and snore so loud he threatened to give away our position, but we were afraid to wake him. The PFs giggled and laughed. It was very embarrassing. When I went back to CACO headquarters I'd find him passed out in his office. In his defense, I knew he was terribly concerned about what was going on. Our CAP in 1970 was making a lot of contact and it worried him. His headquarters was not secured well and he didn't have many men to defend it. There were a bunch of lifer Army people back at headquarters who didn't know the difference between the muzzle and the butt end of a rifle, so security was a Marine responsibility. I'd love to meet the guy today, see how he's doing, tell him it's alright; we all did what we had to do to survive there.

There was only one individual who didn't belong. He'd been with a line company about four months before he joined us and had developed a real hatred for the Vietnamese. He physically and verbally abused them; he was an embarrassment to our CAP. He was a real gutsy guy and terrific in a firefight, but he never should have been placed in the Combined Action Program.

The rest of the guys were a cut above the usual Marine, very motivated with a real esprit de corps. The other services just don't have anywhere near the pride the Marines do. I was envious. As time went on it became infectious and I began to see myself less and less as a Navy corpsman and more and more as a Marine. I had to consciously remind myself that I was a hospital corpsman in the Navy, not a Marine.

We depended on each other. These guys would do anything for me and I would do anything, absolutely anything, for them. We never let each other down. We never smoked dope or got drunk. Nobody did drugs. This was because we were in a very hairy situation. Twenty-four hours a day we had to keep our shit together so we could all get home alive.

I referred to the guys I served with as my Marines, and I was their Doc. To my grave, I will be their Doc.

★　　★　　★

Dr. Wayne Christiansen is an emergency-room physician at the Charlton Memorial Hospital in Fall River, Massachusetts. He lives in Tiverton, Rhode Island, with his family.

Dr. Wayne Christiansen

135

Warren V. Smith

4th CAG
1969

Warren Smith was ordered to South Vietnam in March 1969, where he was assigned as an interpreter and interrogator in various CAPs within 4th CAG.

Interrogators have a bad reputation. People see movies depicting them as animals. I've seen people slapped and punched, but I never saw any electric torture devices or someone thrown out of a helicopter. I'm not saying these things didn't happen; I'm sure they did. But these are poor techniques. Let's say you take two enemy soldiers up in a helicopter and throw one out so the other guy starts talking. What if you take up a colonel and a private? Unknowingly you toss out the colonel. How much information are you going to get out of a private?

With the exception of one guy, all the interrogations I saw or was involved in were successful. They all broke. The real problem was whether or not to believe the information they were giving you. My theory was the NVA and VC purposely left behind shitbirds to tell us lies, or shitbirds who knew nothing or were given false information.

After a month and a half in country I volunteered for a CAP unit. I was in three different CAPs: 4-3-4, 4-3-6, and 4-3-7. My first ville was Van Hoa, just east of Quang Tri City. Up till then no shot had been fired in Van Hoa during the Vietnam War. I still think the village elders, and the villagers themselves, had a deal going with the enemy. The PFs were terrible. They thought their job was to keep everybody away from the women and steal from us. There was quite a bit of frustration and animosity. Older people died because disease was rampant in the village, and it was disappointing because we couldn't get a chopper into the ville to medevac some of these sick people. They were supposed to use Vietnamese assets for this.

I stayed by myself at Van Hoa. The Marines there treated me

kind of funny and I couldn't understand why. Then I learned why—they thought I was a narc! They'd never heard of a Marine interpreter being attached to a CAP. To make matters worse, the company clerk was the one spreading this bullshit! So I went back to headquarters, placed my M-16 across his desk, and said if he continued telling these lies I'd blow his brains out. Thank God I was there for only twenty-one days.

Le Xuyen was my next ville; a CAP had just been established there. It was in an area that had experienced heavy damage during Operation Prairie, and they'd evacuated the villagers. Now they were bringing them back to resettle the place. I remember a pagoda full of holes, and unexploded naval shells just lying all over the place. And the kids were banging on these rounds with rocks, thinking they were toys!

We moved every day. During daylight we cleaned weapons, stayed visible, visited the people, and tried not to act like geeks. Two other Marines and I, Pfc George Benitez, nicknamed Lizard, and Rocky Jay, got bored one day so we went out to these sand dunes sighting in our weapons and trying to shoot down a few birds. On our way back we spotted several Vietnamese women and went over to talk to them. One was blind and they all acted real nervous. We checked their IDs but those things could've easily been faked. I felt something was wrong, so when we returned to the ville I told the CAP leader, Sergeant Nelson, about them. He said the squad was going into the area that night and we'd check it out.

As it got dark, I noticed the kids weren't around. They usually followed us all around, but this time their mothers were calling for them. We should've known something was up then. We reached the last house in this area and began to set up; I put my pack down in this courtyard with my ammo on top of it. We had our PFs with us, who by the way were really good. One of them goes out to this wooded area to take a shit, and suddenly I hear gunfire. The PF's running toward us pulling up his pants and screaming, "VC! VC!"

Everything just erupted; I was next to this PF. When I went to put a fresh magazine into my rifle I noticed I only had three or four rounds in it. I'd forgotten to reload them after the dunes. I ran over to my pack with the ammo on it, which was in the center of this courtyard, but when I turned to run back I was suddenly mesmerized by the war all around me. I don't know what came over me but I just watched the sights and listened to the sounds. A

Warren V. Smith

couple of rounds buzzed by me but I still didn't move. Then the PF I was with dashes over to me and pulls me down and leads me back to our position. He actually ran out there to save my life. He could have hollered to me but he risked his own life by running to me.

A couple of VC tried to outflank us but we opened up on full automatic. I know we hit them both, but when we went out later to check we found blood but no bodies. Finally the enemy withdrew. We had this dog-handler with us from the 101st Airborne and we decided to follow the blood trails. The Trung-si wanted no part of it because he felt the VC would return with a larger force or mortar us if we lingered too long. The Vietnamese sergeant just wanted to get out of the area.

It was dark so we popped a flare, which hit a tree, bounced off, and burned down a nearby hootch. Talk about an embarrassing situation! It didn't do much in the way of winning hearts and minds.

We picked up three VC suspects. One was a woman with two slits for a nose; it really looked disgusting. The Vietnamese had food laid out in their houses; it was so obvious that it was for the VC. I started to question them but the PFs kept kicking them in the side, which prevented me from doing the interrogation properly. So to appease them, I slapped the suspects in the face. Not too hard, but hard enough so that the PFs did stop kicking them. I actually pulled those slaps back on purpose; I didn't want to see these people get hurt unnecessarily. Now I could ask questions and try to get some answers using my own methods without interference from the PFs.

When I was satisfied, the PFs blindfolded and gagged the suspects. Then they strung them together by placing a rope around each of their necks so they couldn't run. When that was done we started to leave. It was a dark, moonless night. I was the second to the last one to depart. We'd gone a short distance when the PF in front of me stops and says he left his bicycle behind. So back he goes and I stand there waiting for him. He forgot to mention that the rest of the unit had kept moving. It was real dark, so I didn't see it. Here I am with three VC suspects and two PFs in an area we'd just been ambushed in not twenty minutes before, and I'm the only American.

I realized I had to reach the other Marines. I told one of the PFs to walk point, but they both had the jitters and refused. So, reluctantly, I walked point, which is something I didn't want to do. I wanted to keep my eye on the whole bunch. I took a chance and walked a bit, stopped, and fired one round from my rifle in the air. Soon I heard the sound of an artillery flare going up, and it lit the area. I moved ahead, real cautiously, and fired another shot and listened. I did this several times, and then I heard a shot in the distance. I felt relieved but then thought to myself, this could be the VC waiting in ambush for me. But I took a chance and went closer. We had a prearranged signal: if you were coming in unanswered, you popped a red flare. So I did it. A few minutes go by and I see a green flare go up, the return signal. It was my CAP! I'd made it back safely.

Since I knew the Vietnamese language, a couple of funny things come to mind. First, *CAC*, loosely translated, means "penis" in Vietnamese. When the program first began it was called a CAC outfit and the Marines would say, "I'm in a CAC." The Vietnamese thought he was saying, "I'm a penis." They thought it was hilarious. That's why they changed it to CAP.

We had a Trung-si whose name was Diet. He'd walk around with a big plastic flower in his hat and make a complete fool out of himself. When the Marines tried to say his name, it came out sounding like Trung-si Anus. Well, the villagers poked fun at him and he got real pissed and waved his .45 all over the place threatening to shoot somebody. Before he lost any more face, I told the guys to stop calling him that.

One of the nicest things about being in a CAP was mingling with the Vietnamese people. I remember one time when some of the Marines and PFs hired a prostitute for the evening. That hooker wasn't in the village an hour when a throng of women gathered around and started protesting her presence there. It was like a rampaging Women's League, Vietnamese style. That prostitute got on the back of a motor scooter and left. They literally ran her out of town.

Schoolteachers and village chiefs were prime targets for assassination. There was one woman who operated a school nearby, so we'd periodically check on her. She lived in a constant state of fear. One night I walked in to see if she was alright and I must've startled her, because her eyes got wide when I stepped into the room. When she saw it was me, you could see the relief on her face. The village chief was so terrified he stayed at Quang Tri City. If the head of the ville didn't feel safe, that meant the area wasn't pacified. If the NVA or VC came into the area to get something to eat or hold indoctrination classes, though, we often heard about it right away. I felt that was progress.

One of the families we occasionally stayed with had a VC son. One evening we set up an ambush in the house hoping to snare him, but the father got out of bed every once in a while and tried to light a candle. Obviously, it was a signal to the son to stay away. We put out the candle and told him to go back to bed. It was sad.

Besides our PFs, there were RFs located nearby. We had a mutual agreement—we hated each other. We almost had a gunfight with them one time. I had gone over to this Vietnamese vendor by the bridge to buy some of those jellied candies wrapped in leaves. Well, one of the RFs stole my bush hat. We began arguing with the RFs at the bridge and pretty soon everybody locked and loaded, but then we calmed down and left. A little while later the VC attacked this bridge and the RFs called for assistance from our CAP. We all just sat around the radio listening and laughing at them. Fortunately, no one was hurt in the attack.

As bad as these RFs were, there was something worse—RDs [Revolutionary Development cadres]. They rode on motor scooters and wore black pajamas; they thought they were hot shit. In my opinion, they were nothing more than a big bunch of draft dodgers. Also, if it wasn't nailed down, they stole it.

One day they robbed all our grenades to go fishing. They tossed them into the river and when they exploded and the stunned fish floated to the surface, they collected the fish and gave them to this young Vietnamese girl so she could cook them. Needless to say, we were pissed. We ran to the river and sprayed insecticide all over the fish and the girl cooking them. That, by the way, was my major atrocity in Vietnam. And that could have avoided if they'd just asked for some grenades. We would've given them some, that is, as long as we got invited to the fish fry.

As the 3d Marine Division was standing down, the U.S. Army began moving into our AO. There was real lack of communication between the CAPs and the Army. A unit of the 1st Brigade, 5th Mechanized Division sometimes operated in our villages.

One day I'm walking down the road and all of a sudden I walked into a company-size sweep! Talk about no communication! At night they ran ambushes in our AO. The Army sent their patrols out by compass: so many degrees, et cetera. We went out by checkpoints: Checkpoint 1 could be a certain house, Checkpoint 2 a pagoda, and so on. On one night ambush, one of their patrols strolled right into our kill zone. We just let them pass; they never knew we were there. If it wasn't for the full moon that night, we would've greased half of them.

You needed a special kind of Marine to be in a CAP. A lot of guys developed an attitude toward the Vietnamese, but a guy like that was very detrimental for a CAP. We had one Marine who always bragged about wanting to shoot somebody. He finally did it one day: he shot this woman in the leg who was out of her hootch after dark. We'd established martial law in our AO—no one out after dark. If anyone had to go to the bathroom, they were supposed to carry a lantern with them. More than likely this old woman forgot the lantern, so he opens fire. This guy didn't belong in a CAP.

I hate to say this, but you had to be a gook lover. That's what they used to call me. I wouldn't say I was a gook lover though, I just treated the Vietnamese the way I'd want to be treated.

We had a caretaker and his family living in one of the houses owned by the Catholic church. He took care of the building and grounds because the parish priest was in Quang Tri and could only get out there once in a while. The guy let us store C-rats there; we did it because we knew he'd watch over them. I went in there one day, started a fire, cooked up some C's, and begin eating. The caretaker came out to see who was there and when he saw it was me I could see he was upset, but he didn't say anything. I started thinking about it. Here's a guy, if caught by the Viet Cong for befriending Americans, would probably be killed, along with his family. Then here comes an uninvited guest into his home who just sits down and eats, doesn't even ask permission. How would you like it if someone barged into your house and did that? So I stopped cooking and cleaned up everything. He was happier than hell.

In 1972, after I was discharged from the Marine Corps, I was watching the evening news. The Easter Offensive had just erupted in Vietnam and they were doing a special report on PFs in the Quang Tri area. That was the scene of heavy fighting in spring '72. I recognized some houses and the terrain from our AO when I was there in '69, and then I saw some of my PFs on TV! The 3d ARVN Division had run, but these guys had stayed and fought. That was an eerie feeling, watching that.

I really believed in the CAPs. I think if we ever get involved in Central America, they should resurrect the program and put more time and effort into it. It would be more beneficial than sending battalions and regiments all over the place looking for the enemy. Let's hope the military learns from the CAP experience in Vietnam.

★   ★   ★

Warren Smith teaches at Monadnock Regional High School in Swanzey, New Hampshire, and is a major in the U.S. Army Reserves attached to Military Intelligence. During the 1991 Gulf crisis, Smith did a short stint on active duty at the Pentagon in Washington, D.C., participating in Operation Desert Shield. He lives in Dublin, New Hampshire, with his wife and their three children.

Gary Kovach

1st CAG
1969–1970

U.S. Navy Corpsman Gary Kovach arrived in Vietnam in November 1969. On May 8, 1970, his CAP, 1-3-2, was assaulted by a large NVA and VC force. His heroic actions on that eventful night earned him the Silver Star Medal, but circumstances surrounding the action have haunted him ever since.

Our CAP was located in a farming community in Quang Ngai Province near a town on Highway 1 called Binh Son. The AO was a valley eight miles by three miles, containing three major villages that had at least two minor hamlets each, all interconnected by a narrow dirt road. The Vietnamese farmers scraped their living from a patchwork of rice paddies, sugar cane, and sweet potatoes. Before my arrival Lt. William Calley and his men had torn up a village about five miles away—My Lai. This caused local hatred and distrust of outsiders.

The Korean Marines also played a role in fostering hostility; their attitude was that this was a token peacekeeping force without a mission, and they sold whatever they could lay their hands on in the local black market.

On May 8, 1970, I awoke suddenly from a deep sleep—something wasn't right. It was 0100. I pulled on a pair of cut-offs and went to the bunker where we kept the radio. Dave Frenier was huddled over a candle flame at an improvised desk. The radio crackled and hissed, and the men on ambush talked very quietly, so I couldn't identify the voice.

I took over the radio watch from Frenier, since I was wide awake. About an hour later I woke up the next radio watch and started back to the radio bunker. All of a sudden the air was full of screaming projectiles and colored tracers. I started running, probably faster than in my entire life. A wave of bodies hit me at the radio-room door, and everybody was confused and scared. They broke for open ground and the trenches.

Gary Kovach

A rocket slammed into the wall opposite where I was standing and I was thrown to the floor. Then I regained my equilibrium and grabbed my rifle, ammunition, bandages, and boots, ran outside, and fell into a trench hole about thirty feet from the building. All I had on was cut-offs. Outside my hole there was just darkness filled with enemy rifle fire. The mortars and rockets had let up but I didn't hear our return fire.

I looked over the edge as a flare went up and saw a Nghia Quan engaged in hand-to-hand combat with an unfamiliar Vietnamese. Then the flare took a dive into a rice paddy. Pretty soon another flare went up and I saw several Vietnamese dressed in black coming through the barbed wire.

I look down the barrel of my rifle but I am frozen. I can't react. Can't blow them away. I'm frantic with indecision. Then my moment to act is gone; the flare's light fades. I would kill them today if I had that chance again, but I can't go back.

Another flare goes up and I watch two men in the hole opposite mine plunge down into the pit, their hands on each other's throats. Then one overpowers the other, knifes him in the throat, and throws the body over the edge and down the embankment, out of sight.

The next time I pop my head up, it's just in time to see a grenade launched in my direction. I bury my head in my ass and pray the thrower never played baseball. Thank God the grenade falls short.

Infiltrators are still picking their way through the wire, but I can't take the outright initiative to gun them down. Time seems suspended and I watch the figures move in slow motion through the wire in my direction. Finally I fire my rifle and watch my rounds make contact, causing their bodies to jerk as if jolted by electricity.

Suddenly I'm flung head over heels by an exploding grenade. Within seconds I'm staring into the vacant sky flat on my back. I manage to slip into a hole next to a Marine named Erky. I check myself to see if everything's there. Keith, the machine gunner, is lying facedown in the trench.

"Is he . . . " I can't bring myself to ask the question.

"Naw, scared!" Erky says. "They're gonna overrun us, Doc!"

I say no way, but then Erky tells me Sarge and Dave are in the bunker on the radio; Pina and Tim are in the far trench behind Kentucky and Bo; and he hasn't seen Jones at all.

I grab Keith from the bottom of the pit and scream at him, "Goddamn it, Keith, get up! Do you want to die in this shit at the hands of these lousy bastards? Aren't you a Marine?"

An ear-shattering explosion tears apart the church—a satchel charge. Their infiltration of our defenses is nearly complete, and if we don't do something we'll all be killed.

I notice a group of VC near our abandoned command post. I pull my rifle over the edge of the trench, level my sights at them, and squeeze the trigger. Nothing. I've run out of ammunition. I feel doomed.

Then I hear an enraged scream followed by a volley of automatic-weapons fire. The rounds find their mark in the group of enemy soldiers. Keith is now marching toward me with the M-60 braced against his hip and the ammunition belt slung across his shoulder. He keeps advancing, firing volley after volley. He seems to have no fear.

I turn to welcome him into the trench, but he collapses on top of me. I try to get him out of the hole but I can't maneuver him. With one hand I search his body for the bullet hole and with the other I locate a bandage. I have to move him to a better position to properly bandage the wound.

Then I realize Keith's blood is running down my legs and covering my arms. It has a sweet smell. I cry out, "God in heaven, if you exist, help me save this boy's life!"

Suddenly Keith is awake and full of panic. His hands begin raking my face and pulling at my clothes. He grabs my throat and his fingernails cut deep into my neck. He's seized by a coughing fit and is now choking in his own blood. The wound is under his left rib cage, and I know the blood will soon fill the left lung cavity. There's no way I can get a medevac chopper in, but I will not accept this defeat and I try desperately to save him.

I search for a pulse and locate a faint throb in the femoral artery. I flip Keith onto his good side to give him at least one lung to breathe with. Then I feel him shudder and his body becomes calm. I look up to see that Pina, Erky, Jones, and Kentucky have gathered around and witnessed Keith's death.

And there is no God.

Then Jones and I furiously send volley after volley of 60-mm mortar fire into our perimeter. Now the mortar ammo's running low and the rest of the rounds are stored in a back room of the CP. I get out of the mortar pit and make a run for the door. The room is unchanged and unoccupied. I pull a case of mortar ammo out of the locker and instinctively turn because I feel the presence of someone behind me. I see a figure outlined in the back doorway and we stand looking at each other. He doesn't do anything to stop me so I run back to the mortar pit.

I remember thinking, Why didn't he stop me? Why did he let me escape? Did he recognize me? Was he a local village VC sympathizer who's known me from my work in the village and let me get away because I helped him in the past?

The wounded are laid out along the trench line, and I work on them for over an hour applying dressings and giving reassurances. The Vietnamese have taken the worse of it; the VC had to break through the PF's lines before hitting ours.

The Nghia Quan's wounds are horrendous. One young Vietnamese boy got a round through his gut that drew the intestines up over his chest like a bouquet of flowers. And now he's awake to talk about it. Another lost an arm to a grenade blast and is learning to smoke with the other while waiting for a medevac chopper. Still another has been hit in the face but is conscious enough to ask about the condition of the Marines. I am amazed by the resilience and fortitude of these people.

I stand up and look down the row of men. They're all looking at me and I feel good. I stoop to pick up my rifle and this one Vietnamese grabs my arm. I look into the man's eyes and read what the PF can't say. In spite of our loss, I've saved as many as I could. I did my best. I place my hand on his.

Now I walk with renewed strength to the machine-gun bunker. The early morning light gives me an advantage and I see the VC crawling along the paths between the rice paddies. I find an M-79 grenade launcher and begin to lob rounds at the retreating enemy. Word came down later that I was right on target. Then we hear the Army's sending in reinforcements that'll arrive within the hour.

I have asked myself again and again if things would have been different if I hadn't forced Keith out of hiding. Would they have overrun our position if he hadn't reacted? Would I have been killed in that hole like the Nghia Quan if Keith hadn't come? Would he or any of us be alive today?

I lost count of the choppers that came, but the number of wounded was sixteen Nghia Quans injured and evacuated. We lost one Marine and six Nghia Quans to sixty-nine VC.

I walked over to where Keith's body lay. Ants were crawling on his face, and I hollered for someone to bring me a poncho liner or something to cover him. I tried not to cry and asked where Keith's chopper was. Someone said no chopper would take him; they all had urgent missions.

I grabbed the radio handset and screamed, "This is Buggy Treaty 2 to any overhead traffic!"

There was no answer and I repeated the call. This time someone answered. "This is Airvac 1, come in, over."

"Roger, Airvac 1. We need an airlift for a Kilo-India-Alpha, over."

"Sorry, Buggy Treaty 2. Not heading back to base hospital at this time."

I pleaded. "You must make this trip for a fallen American!"

There was a long pause and then he said, "Roger, Buggy Treaty 2. Coming down."

I helped to carry more than twenty bodies to the choppers that day, but Keith's I wanted to carry alone. I pulled him close to me as I stood. As I walked to the chopper, the wind blew the poncho off and unveiled Keith's face. I started to cry.

As the bird lifted off, I took two steps back and turned to watch. The wind hurt but I took the beating as the price to pay for watching Miguel Keith's body fly off. I still live with the memory of a man who died trying to save the lives of his friends. My life changed forever.

For his heroic actions that night, L. Cpl. Miguel Keith was awarded a Medal of Honor. He was the only CAP Marine in the Vietnam War to receive our nation's highest decoration.

★　　★　　★

Gary Kovach was awarded the Silver Star, the Navy Commendation Medal, the Purple Heart, and the Combat Action Ribbon while serving in a CAP in Vietnam from 1969 to 1970. He is married with two sons and lives in Ohio.

Capt. Tom Moore, USMC (Ret.)

CAF Headquarters
1969–1970

Enlisting in the Marine Corps in 1951 at age seventeen, Missouri native Tom Moore made it his career. His first tour in Vietnam was with 3d Tank Battalion, and in his second tour he was assigned the frustrating task of supply officer for the Combined Action Force until its stand-down in 1970.

I can say in all honesty that my tour of duty as the CAF S-4 officer is the one I take the most pride in.

I was assigned to CAG Headquarters in September 1969 as the S-4—supply officer. I had to fight city hall to have priority requisitions filled, and I seldom won those fights. Certain items were in short supply at all times, like batteries for starlight scopes and strobe lights.

I'm sure we were on the low end of the customer list at FLC [Force Logistics Command]; the infantry regiments had priority over us. However, due to the lobbying of our CO, Col. Ted Metzger, the Combined Action Program eventually became the Combined Action Force. Colonel Metzger was able to go from being a chief of staff in charge of a program to CO of a unit with, theoretically, 6,000 men under arms, including the PFs. Once we were designated a force, our supply posture improved.

I had six Marines and eighteen Vietnamese working for me at CAF headquarters. We had a truck driver with us, a black Marine by the name of Joe Nathan MacFarland, from Jackson, Mississippi. He would go to FLC at Red Beach with a few requisitions and a shopping list. Sometimes he got the requisitions filled, but he never failed to complete his shopping list. Once Colonel Metzger asked for some of the new Army-type rucksacks and Joe went straight to the Army's 80th Logistical Force Command. He came back with a six-by filled with the rucksacks. And I don't recall his leaving the compound with anything to trade.

As for the Vietnamese, from a supply viewpoint, the PFs really

Capt. Tom Moore

liked illumination. An S-4 officer for one of the CAGs gave this explanation: "Those PF bastards won't move unless we light up the area like San Antonio on a Saturday night."

Among the Vietnamese with me was a Master Sergeant Hung, a twelve-year veteran of the ARVN. He was on the staff at I Corps headquarters and was sent to me TAD [temporarily attached duty]. He was a real hot dog. His English was just as good as, if not better than, some of the CAP Marines'. He accompanied us on all our MEDCAP operations from CAF headquarters. He did an excellent job as an interpreter. Hung was married to a half-French, half-Vietnamese woman, a real looker. She was a secretary for the U.S. Army Special Forces headquarters in Da Nang. She also had a good command of the English language.

For a long time I had a sneaking suspicion that Hung and his wife were deeply involved with the black market, but this was not confirmed until we were preparing to leave Vietnam. All the CAP units had been deactivated by this time, except 2d CAG. We were deactivating the CAF headquarters, and Hung contacted me at my quarters. It was an unforgettable scene. He literally got down on his knees with tears in his eyes and his hands folded in prayer, and begged me to find a way for him and his wife to leave Vietnam. He told me word was out in the neighborhood that there was a contract on their lives, and it would be filled as soon as we were out of the area. This was for four reasons: he and his wife worked directly for the Americans, they were both Catholic, all members of the I Corps staff were to be eliminated, and he'd been making a big profit on the black market.

I never did find out what happened to them. I don't know how one would go about getting information on a member of the South Vietnamese Army; God knows it's hard enough to find out what happened to some of the Americans who served there. It's nearly impossible to get any information through our own government.

The South Vietnamese government was corrupt, and Hung was a good case in point. There were some dedicated people driven by a feeling of nationalistic pride, but most of the field grade officers under General Lam at I Corps were just a bunch of fat cats. I feel very strongly that the South Vietnamese government was destroyed from within by the self-serving attitude of those entrusted to save their country.

But the Combined Action Program did its job. We had outstanding Marines in the program, due in great part to Capt. Norbert "Ski" Norwicki. He was responsible for maintaining quality within the TO/E. I knew him from Warrant Officer School, where we were classmates in 1961. He spoke five or six languages and was a dedicated officer and a real intellectual.

Ski or his S-1 chief would meet all incoming flights at the reception center in Da Nang, and they would screen service-record books of arriving Marines. I sincerely believe that because of Ski's efforts, the CAP Marine was a cut above the average grunt in the line companies.

The CAP concept worked. The Marines, both officers and enlisted, made it work. And it might be the only thing over there that really did work.

★   ★   ★

Retiring from active duty in 1974, Tom Moore became a police officer at the age of forty. He has risen to the rank of Deputy Chief of Police for Roeland Police Department in Roeland, Kansas. He is the co-author of two books: Green Side Out, Marine Corps Sea Stories *and* The Raggedy-Ass Marines *(Blountstown, Fla.: Gayle Publishers, 1980, 1981). He and his wife, Lee, have been married for thirty-four years and have four children.*

Maj. H. G. Duncan, USMC (Ret.)

4th CAG
1970

Enlisting in February 1950, Maj. H. G. Duncan served as an infantryman and Russian linguist until his discharge in 1954. He remained in the Reserves and later reentered the regular Marine Corps as a 2d lieutenant in 1961. He served two tours in South Vietnam and was wounded twice.

In September 1969 I returned to South Vietnam as a tank officer. In early 1970 plans were implemented for a drawdown. With most of my tour still to serve, I applied for duty with the Combined Action Force. I was accepted [one of the few noninfantry personnel in the CAF] and assigned to the 4th Combined Action Group in Quang Tri.

Our area of operations was in the northern portion of the I Corps TAOR; we had twelve to fifteen CAPs operating in this area. My position with the 4th CAG was S-3 officer. Later, as we began to deactivate, I also became the group executive officer.

Some PFs were devoted to the CAP, but others had "accommodations" with the VC. I knew none who exuded any patriotism to South Vietnam as a country. If the CAP had a strong leader, he commanded the respect and admiration—almost devotion—of the PFs. But even then, PFs would often attempt to avoid battle. A specific example of this was in CAP 4-1-2, led by one of the finest CAP Marines I knew: nineteen-year-old Brice Romo of Montana. He scored many successes in the few months I was with 4th CAG. Romo advised me that he was not getting the cooperation he expected from his PF platoon sergeant, so I told him to plan a good day patrol and I'd go along. He had reliable intelligence telling him the VC had positions in a particular location, so we set out from the day haven on a direct course to the area. The PF platoon sergeant got increasingly nervous the closer we got. Finally he started off on a tangent with his platoon, saying, "VC this way." I allowed Romo to retain command, but I did interject that we were to stay on the original course. The PF platoon sergeant argued, and finally he broke off his men and returned to the day haven, leaving the Marines to continue on alone. It turned out to be a walk in the sun, with no hostile contact. But this told me that the PF did have an accommodation with the enemy. He thought the enemy was where Romo wanted to go and he had no desire to engage them.

Another night a PF fired a flare at the most inopportune time and against fire-discipline orders. He thought it was funny, and the acting CAP leader told me that was about routine for his CAP. I asked him why the problem had not been reported to me, the operations officer, earlier. He said he'd been told not to report negative things about the PFs. Faults of the PFs were often overlooked at that time, but reports made by Marines were viewed with suspicion and disbelief. I tried to be philosophical in my pessimism and decided that even if the PFs were useless, at least they were occupied and not fighting for the enemy.

The 4th CAG was totally in the TAOR of the U.S. Army units. Headquarters was in the middle of the Army compound that had originally been the headquarters of the 3d Marine Division. As operations officer, I attended daily briefings for the Army commanding general. It appeared that the CAPs were having significantly more contact with the enemy than the Army was, especially starting in May 1970, and the general praised us for our successes.

We were about 90 percent dependent on the Army for logistics support and 100 percent for artillery and medevac support. They were absolutely magnificent. Artillery was timely and accurate, and the helicopter medevacs were flown by young Army warrant officers who seemed totally without fear. When I was first assuming my duties, I went to the dust-off pilots and asked what they needed from the ground. A young pilot, probably about twenty years old, said, "The truth." I asked him what he meant, and he said they were often told the landing zone was cold, when in fact it was hot. He said, "We'll go in, hot or cold, but we need to know."

Army medical treatment of Marines and PFs was also excellent. The Army did their level best to support the CAPs in the 4th CAG. I think they, if no one else, got the real picture of the hardships the CAPs were enduring. While I was with 4th CAG, the III

Maj. H. G. Duncan (left)

MAF turned over command to the Army's XXIV Corps, but I saw no letup in Marine Corps support to the CAGs.

Some of the Army personnel in district level headquarters were Special Forces. They had the equipment and maybe the personnel to do what we were doing, but we did it better. Generally speaking, they were not at all helpful.

If there was a weakness, it was in the selection and training of CAP Marines. The CAF adjutant screened service records of incoming Marines who had infantry MOSs, and he generally had his pick of the crop. He did well, but I think the criteria for selecting them was missing. The essential requirement was that they be 100 percent volunteers, only after a comprehensive briefing of what CAP duty consisted of. But CAP casualties were high, and the tendency seemed to be to hide this fact from the incoming CAP Marines.

They were trained by a CAF school where the emphasis was on "understanding" the Vietnamese culture. For example, if a PF steals your radio, don't get mad—he doesn't have one. There wasn't enough emphasis on squad tactics and combat situations. Also, I was not impressed with the attitudes and qualifications of the instructors at the school. Personally, I think the Marine Corps should have identified and trained CAP Marines before shipping them to South Vietnam. Then a short in-country course would have been enough.

When I had about thirty days left in country, I was assigned a special project of teaching night-firing and quick-kill techniques. This particular CAG—one of the three left—was having a lot of contacts but very few kills. I found out why.

I instructed one CAG per day, taking a good supply of ammo and spare weapons to the site. Before doing anything else I'd inspect the weapons and question the personnel, especially the CAP leader. I was appalled to find that many CAPs had ordnance that did not function. This included more than half the claymore mines (they had bad electric circuits) and a few machine guns. CAP leaders, for the most part, had no idea how to test the circuits on the claymore mines, and none of them had a circuit tester. One CAP leader said he'd called in about a malfunctioning machine gun every day for over a month. These Marines were taking this faulty ordnance on ambush sites and patrols.

Overall, I would rate that CAG as incapable of performing its mission. I found a widespread lack of discipline, particularly in one company that had poor leadership at the top. There was hostility between Marines and PFs in almost all the CAPs. Once we got started on the marksmanship training, though, interest increased, and the Marines seemed to want to do well. I think the fact that someone had come out to assist them improved morale. And I'm not saying this to be self-serving.

One of the company commanders was provided my schedule for his CAPs and gave almost no cooperation. He looked at my project as just spying and fault-finding to be reported to the CAF commander. But that was not the case. The CAF commander and I had agreed that I would go to the field, identify the problem, and correct it. Then I would simply report it corrected—no details. And that is what happened.

So most of the lack of Marine Corps cooperation for the CAPs seemed to be internal. But for the most part the CAP Marines were good, as their success rate shows. The high casualty rate caused a sense of resignation, a kind of let's-get-on-with-it attitude, and also an atmosphere of apprehension. This kept Marines from doing all they could to be successful in combat.

In addition, a big problem all the military services had to contend with was what was known as Project 100,000. Secretary of Defense Robert McNamara created it to assist President Lyndon Johnson's Great Society efforts. The military was directed to take into its ranks Category IV recruits and draftees who normally would have been excluded because of low intelligence, behavior patterns, police problems, and so on. And some of these people inevitably found their way into the CAPs, which did not help matters.

We were also frustrated because the majority of Vietnamese would not cooperate with us by telling where the VC were located and where they had last been in the village. We failed to realize that the rural Vietnamese were also victims of the VC, and the VC were much more pointed in their dealings with them. They threatened to kill any village chief or villager who cooperated with the Americans, and they often punctuated their demands by inflicting mayhem.

With the mobile CAPs, the VC and NVA never knew where the Marines would be unless something had been compromised. I suspect this happened in far too many cases, but once bloodied, the CAP Marines seemed to take on the instincts of hunters hungry for game. And this mind-set was a necessity for great success.

Ambushes were planned no more than a day ahead of time and the PFs were not told about them until it was time to go. Discipline on ambushes was good. It was my unscientific observation that the country boys made the best ambush Marines, as the ones raised in the city seemed to get fidgety very quickly.

I think the CAP program was the most successful thing we had going in Vietnam, but I also think too much emphasis was placed on not offending the people we were protecting. We expected tact and diplomacy from young American Marines who did not possess such qualifications, nor had they been trained for such a mission.

But I know of no other Marine Corps unit that lived as they did, suffered the privations they did, or had the success they did—even if the individual successes were small.

* * *

Since his retirement in 1979, Maj. H. G. Duncan has lived in Blounts-town, Florida, where he operates his own publishing firm, Gayle Pub-lishers. He has written and published several books dealing with Marine Corps life, *including:* Scream and Shout *(1983)*, Dunk's Almanac *(1981)*, The Second Wind *(1987)*, Renegade by Choice *(1989)*, The Birth of Clint McQuade *(1988)*, Clint McQuade, USMC *(1990)*, and The Benevolent Curmudgeon *(1992)*.

Maj. H. G.
Duncan

157

Art Falco

1st and 2d CAG
1970

Connecticut native Artie Falco spent twelve months with two different CAGs in 1970. He served with CAPs 1-2-1 and 2-3-7.

I had already served eighteen months in country as a helicopter door gunner in the U.S. Army with the 48th Assault Helicopter Company. After I was discharged I enlisted in the Marine Corps and signed a waiver to go back to Vietnam as a CAP Marine.

At CAP school graduation they played the theme song from *The Magnificent Seven,* which seemed like an appropriate song because, just like in the movie, we had to teach the villagers to defend themselves against the bad guys so they could farm in peace.

Later I ran into a friend of mine, Bernie Russell from Baltimore, Maryland, who asked if I wanted to get in his unit. He said he knew the first sergeant and could get me transferred to his CAP in 1st CAG. Luckily I didn't go, because his CAP, south of Tam Ky, got wiped out. They were in their day site when three VC just happened to walk in on them and then took off running. The Marines chased them while the PFs stayed at the day site guarding the gear. Those Marines ran right into a company-size ambush. Nine were killed; the only one to escape was the radio operator, who floated facedown in the river pretending to be dead. The VC even took the radio off his back. A friend of mine in CAP headquarters, Jim Field from Bristol, Connecticut, said Bernie got shot in the head at close range.

I stayed with 1st CAG for about six months. I was in 1-2-1, south of Tam Ky, just north of Chu Lai. We stayed east of the Red Line, or Highway 1. It was usually pretty quiet, but one night ambush sticks in my mind. We had three Marines and nine or ten PFs on it. At about 2200 all hell broke loose. Tracers were going off everywhere. Then after a couple of minutes everything just stopped. The PFs were going on a sweep, so I sort of volunteered for it. We got behind this mound and all of a sudden the Trung-si starts barking commands to the PFs. They fix bayonets and then charge over the top of this mound, yelling and screaming like Japanese in a banzai charge, right into this tree line. As I was running, my ankle caught a strand of barbed wire and I fell. I landed on my head, rolled a bit, and came back up, staying right on line with the PFs! But my rifle barrel was caked with dirt. I was lucky no VC were in the tree line, because if I'd had to fire my weapon it probably would've exploded.

Around June 1970 1st CAG was deactivated, and I was transferred to 2d CAG, headquartered at Hoi An.

I knew my buddy Jim Field had gone to 9th Company in 2d CAG, so I asked to be assigned to 9th Company. Then I found out they were near An Hoa in the Arizona Territory, always under attack and constantly being mortared. It looked like another fine mess I had gotten myself into, but the next morning when we received our assignments I was pleasantly surprised to find out I was going to 3d Company at Dien Ban. I decided not to make an issue out of my request for 9th Company.

I went to CAP 2-3-7, about fifteen miles southwest of Da Nang. There were two main villes there: Phong Ngu 1 on the east side, and Phong Ngu 2 on the west side.

There was a lot of VC activity in this area. Before I arrived, 2-3-7 had been virtually wiped out; the Marines had been playing volleyball in this school yard when a couple of kids tossed some grenades at them.

We patrolled constantly, and soon I knew the AO very well. Also, the PFs at 2-3-7 were much better than at 1-2-1. They were really motivated. One of them had been an ARVN paratrooper but had broken his leg and had to take a medical discharge.

The VC seemed to really enjoy tossing grenades at us. During one heavy rain we took a few grenades at our night site and me and another Marine, Joe Majeski from Chicago, took off to man our M-60. As we dove for the weapon we both slid in the mud, right past it. We had to crawl backward about five yards or so to reach the machine gun. Joe got a shrapnel wound that creased his head; nothing serious, but we medevaced him anyway to be treated in the rear. It was his birthday the next day. My flak jacket was full of shrapnel but I didn't get a scratch.

On another night ambush grenades were flung inside our perimeter—two PFs were killed. That's the night I learned to really appreciate helicopter gunships. We were crouched down behind a paddy dike as they were firing their mini-guns and rockets fifteen to twenty yards in front of us. You want them close, but that was too close for me! We went on a sweep for bodies, but as usual we found nothing.

We learned one good lesson: if you leave with ten PFs on patrol, make damn sure you have ten with you all the time! We were setting up an ambush outside this hootch one night, and as we were taking off our packs and getting ready, one of the Marines pointed at a Vietnamese and said, "Hey, he doesn't look familiar!" With that the individual bolted from the group, dropping a grenade. Fortunately no one was hit. We figured he was a VC who'd been inside the hootch taking a nap, not realizing we'd taken up positions outside. Then he'd attempted to blend in with the PFs, realizing he was completely surrounded. Well, the old saying they all look alike didn't work that time. We knew our PFs.

Another night we were at our site when I spotted three VC walking right down Highway 1. It was stupid on their part, plus it was a moonlit evening. I was manning an M-60 and sat quietly waiting for them to get closer. My assistant gunner, Mattson from Massachusetts, whispered in my ear, "Open up!" But I wanted them closer. I didn't want to miss. The next thing I know he's grabbing the gun and pretty soon we're both exchanging fists. Of course, the VC heard us and took off.

One day we had a sergeant from the rear come out to our CAP because he wanted to go on patrols and ambushes. We went through a cemetery on a hill about fifteen feet high. We began searching the graves, explaining to the sergeant that the VC used false graves to hide their food and weapons.

While I was talking to him, the rest of the patrol moved down the hill toward this hootch. As we followed them, I saw a Vietnamese man run from the hootch. My first thought was that the guys had harassed him and he took off. But then I realized the patrol was on the opposite side of the hootch and hadn't seen this guy at all. I immediately started firing and he began to zigzag to avoid the rounds. He made it to the tree line and disappeared just as I finished my magazine. I yelled, "Dung lai!" which means "halt." The sergeant turned to me saying, "Weren't you supposed to yell stop before you started firing?"

By this time the rest of the patrol was in hot pursuit. I hollered to them, "You might be running into an ambush!" They all came to a quick halt at the same time and we proceeded with caution, but we never found him.

One night on ambush, we got a radio message that between 600 and 800 NVA were moving through our area. We were set up and couldn't go anywhere. I was terrified: my whole life flashed before my eyes. Then my Marine Corps training took over and I became real calm. I fixed my bayonet to the end of my rifle, placed my grenades around me, and said to myself, if I'm going to die, I'll take ten of the bastards with me in final hand-to-hand combat. Well, they never appeared. Maybe they changed direction or maybe it was a false report, I'll never know. But I was kind of disappointed. My adrenaline had been pumping and I felt I'd been cheated out of dying in a blaze of glory.

As if patrolling and ambushes weren't enough, somebody came up with the idea of starting a KT—killer team. The concept was to travel light: no pack, flak jacket, helmet, or radio. We wore black pajamas that one of the mama-sans had made for us, and we carried an M-16 with two or three magazines and a few grenades. The team went out on moonless nights to check out hootches where people were known to have VC relatives. Also, sometimes we established a position on a trail to watch and listen. If we did discover any VC, we didn't ambush them. Instead, we followed them and lobbed a few grenades and took off.

Our CAP pulled about six KTs before people in the rear found out about it. KTs were against regulations and we received a message for the guilty parties to cease doing them immediately. They were uneventful, but I'm sure the VC knew about them and I think it kept the enemy off balance for a while. In fact, it might have been the VC who turned us in and had our KTs banned.

Most of the Marines I was with in CAP were damn good, but we had this one new guy who was real gung ho. He wanted us to lay in the rice paddies underwater, breathing through straws. Then, as the VC passed by, we'd jump up and kill them with our K-bars. *Right!*

He ended up being medevaced on his birthday. We had a bunch of new people on a day patrol and sent them out with a couple of experienced guys to get to know the AO. The rest of us set up our day site and guarded the gear. There were three checkpoints we used. We would radio in when we reached them to let the others know everything was alright. The first one was a Buddhist temple we referred to as Buddha. Well, this guy steps on a toe-popper and

Art Falco

161

the radio operator, who was also new, says "booby trap" over the radio. We were laying around playing cards or something, and we thought he said "Buddha." We told him okay, continue on to the next checkpoint. So he comes back and says, "Shouldn't I call in a medevac?" When he said that we all stopped and said, "*Medevac!* What's he talkin' about?" We got out there and found this guy wounded. What was funny about this incident was he'd stepped on a toe-popper, but instead of losing some toes, it had blown off the back of his heel. He was sent to the *Repose* or *Sanctuary*, one of the hospital ships offshore. I remember yelling at him before he left, "You're so fucked up you can't even step on a toe-popper right, asshole!"

One day we found a booby-trapped 105-mm round on a paddy dike. When the villagers went out in the morning to work the fields, we followed them. This particular morning they got off that dike and walked around part of it, then stepped back on again. It was very noticeable. Sure enough, there was the howitzer shell. It hadn't been completely wired up yet; it was probably going to be command-detonated. And it was definitely meant for us.

The villagers were the ones I felt sorry for. They didn't tell us that 105-mm round was there, but I can't blame them. If they'd told us they would've had to deal with the VC. By not telling us, they had to deal with us. And we were the better choice. It was a no-win situation for them. They didn't care who won the war: they were caught in the middle. The villagers just wanted peace.

There was, and still is, quite a bit of prejudice toward the Vietnamese. Our corpsman, John Salinger, tried to get a glass eye for this Vietnamese kid by going through all the proper channels, but he was refused. Then we heard about this West German hospital near Da Nang. It just so happened that our doc was from Pennsylvania Dutch country and spoke German. So the doc, the Vietnamese youngster, and I start hitchhiking down Highway 1. You'd be surprised at the number of vehicles that stopped and said, "We'll give you a ride, but not him." As it turned out we couldn't get him the glass eye, but we did get a nice German meal out of the trip. He was disappointed, but he knew we'd done our best.

In some ways the war was stupid. There was this ARVN compound near Thanh Quit Bridge, which we happened to be near. The Marines getting overrun called for some illum [illumination], and the ARVNs only put up a round every two minutes or so. So another Marine and I jumped into the mortar pit and started putting them up faster. What we didn't know was the ARVNs had an allotment, and once they used up their supply of illumination rounds, they couldn't get more until the next month. The other Marine and I must have used up two weeks' worth of shells. That's no way to fight a war, rationing supplies like that.

I took part in one large operation—well, pretty large for a CAP—while I was in 2-3-7. It involved my CAP and CAP 2-3-8, and U.S. Army helicopters.

We received intelligence reports that high-ranking NVA and VC officers were using the village of Thanh Quit 4 as an R and R center. They'd arrive in the village around six o'clock in the evening and depart around four in the morning, because they knew we always attacked at dawn. To fool them, we assaulted the ville at seven o'clock that night. The plan was to catch them napping and capture or eliminate as many as we could. CAP 2-3-8 was to sweep the ville while we were to act as a blocking force. We called the op Guess Who's Coming to Dinner?

As soon as the choppers landed I saw people running around in the ville. Our CAP had pulled patrols in this AO before, and I'd never seen anybody running like that. I fired the opening shots at the Battle of Thanh Quit 4. We weren't supposed to fire unless fired upon, but I saw this Vietnamese guy wearing white pajamas and hauling ass away from us, so I shot at him as soon as we jumped off the chopper. But I missed. Because 2-3-8 was still a half mile away or so, 2-3-7 became the attacking force. We got credit for one kill; our M-79 man got him. The Huey gunship got twenty-two or twenty-three confirmed KIAs who were trying to cross the river, and we later heard they were in fact high-ranking officers. It turned out to be a real successful op.

During the monsoon season in October 1970, we were hit by a typhoon and our whole AO started going underwater. We started moving toward the Red Line, because it was an all-weather road that had been built up for such emergencies. I had never seen so many snakes in my entire life. As they swam by they tried to climb on us, and so we literally had to shoot our way to the Red Line.

By nightfall we found a dry house. Except for an area of about twenty-five by forty feet, we were completely surrounded by water. As I'm taking off my pack, I hear this hollering and shooting. I look out to see seven or eight Marines on line firing at something, and then I see what it is—the biggest snake I've ever seen! It was brown and yellow and moved up and down in the water like a sea serpent. It had to be a python. It stopped about ten feet from the house as I pulled the pin on a grenade, ready to throw it. Just then it sank and we never saw it again.

The rain kept coming, and finally the Red Line began to get flooded. Helicopters were arriving and evacuating the CAPs, but we had to wait our turn. We moved to the highest ground we knew of in the area, the Thanh Quit Bridge. When the CH-53 finally showed up, the water was up to our waists. There had to be a hundred people on that chopper—villagers, Marines, chickens, goats, pigs. But we escaped. For a minute there I thought we were going to drown.

They took us to LZ Baldy to dry out and we stayed for about a week. It was great! We snuck into a movie one night. Some engineer outfit was showing this English film, but they were only allowing Marines from their unit to enter. We waited until the picture started and went in. We took a PF named Mau with us who'd never seen a movie before. We dressed him in Marine jungle utilities, pulled the cap down low on him, and told him not to talk or smile because of all his gold teeth. We told him he was Italian and his name was Guiseppe. It was dark and we got away with it until Mau started asking questions. He couldn't understand what was going on and we kept telling him to shut up. Finally someone says, "Hey, there's a gook in here!" Everybody started looking around, so we started looking around too. I've never understood why they didn't just turn the lights on. We would have been caught for sure.

It was customary to be pulled out of the bush for your last ten days in country, and everyone looked forward to it because there were supposedly three hot meals, a cot, no work details, and a movie every night.

Well, that wasn't the case when we arrived. Dien Ban, our rear area, had gone under during the flood and had to be rebuilt. And we were the manpower.

We arrived sometime in the afternoon, filled sandbags, had C-rations for supper, and there was no movie because there was no electricity. The next morning we ate C-rations for breakfast, filled sandbags, and had C-rations for lunch. I started to take a nap when Jimmy Field told me we had to dig a head. I said, "That's it! I'm going back to my village. Call me when the plane's ready."

I grabbed my rifle, put on my gear, and walked out of the compound. I flagged down an ARVN soldier riding a Honda and told him to take me to Phong Ngu. Everybody was surprised to see me; we'd said our good-byes the day before. I spent the next week or so in my ville going on patrols and ambushes. Finally I got a call from Jimmy, who said the plane was arriving the next day. I said good-bye to my CAP for the last time and returned to the rear. I don't know how Jimmy did it, but he covered for me all that time. The rear never knew I was back in the bush.

I spent thirty months in Vietnam: eighteen as a door gunner on a Huey and twelve as a CAP Marine. My time in the CAP was definitely the most rewarding.

Art Falco

★　★　★

Artie Falco lives in Littleton, Colorado, where he is employed as a nursing assistant in surgical intensive care at the Denver Veteran's Hospital. He is attending school to become a registered nurse.

Warren Carmon

2d CAG
1970–1971

Warren Carmon did not volunteer for duty with the Combined Action Program. He, like other Marines who went to Vietnam in the 1969–1971 time frame, was sent right from staging battalion to his unit. Carmon spent all of his time in various CAPs within the 2d CAG, near Da Nang.

Ambushes, ambushes, ambushes. It seems like that's all we did in the CAPs I was in. Our group ran them seven nights a week. My God, even the grunts got a chance to go to the rear for some rest.

Some of our ambushes were very successful. Like one night an NVA patrol, fourteen soldiers, entered our killing zone. It was perfect. We opened up on them, dropping eleven instantly. The other three tried to run but never made it.

On the other hand, one night we were down to only two or three people who weren't dead or wounded. I remember reading about it in the *Stars and Stripes*: "Marine casualties moderate; PF casualties light." Right. The PFs had bugged out on us.

I know of some CAPs that sandbagged ambushes [faked patrols]. This was a very, very dangerous thing to do. We did it once. We went to this small RF compound instead of going to our ambush site. So what happens—the enemy hits the compound. We lost a few men that night, but we dealt the VC a big surprise because they didn't know we were there. We never bagged another ambush again.

After a while we got to know our AO pretty good. Sometimes we caught the enemy with his pants down. On one patrol we discovered a large NVA staging area through our starlight scope, and we watched for about an hour as more and more NVA kept arriving. I estimated the group to be about seventy or eighty. So we radioed for artillery. They said they couldn't give it to us because we were too close to a friendly ville. So we asked for mortars. Couldn't get them for the same reason. They finally agreed to send in a gunship. But it never came. Finally we asked what they wanted us to do. They wanted us to engage the enemy! We looked at each other in amazement. There were seventy or eighty of them and ten or twelve of us! Also, the enemy had three machine guns set up on a river, which also served as a natural trench line.

We knew there was an RF compound nearby that had machine guns in the towers. We realized they were out of range, but at least we could disturb the NVA's little party. And when those guns opened up, it did shake 'em up. They knew somebody had been watching 'em. Before they left, though, their guns opened up on us. Green tracers were skipping all over the place. I just hugged the ground, and luckily nobody was hit. That was an interesting night.

I was in three different CAPs: 2-1-1, 2-1-3, and 2-1-5. All of them were located southwest of Da Nang. We were mobile; we had to be to stay alive. The 2d CAG was the hot spot. I think 80 percent of guys that graduated from CAP school wound up there. Booby traps were a real problem.

We'd go out on what they called killer teams, usually three or four guys. What we would do is take an interpreter with us, sneak into a ville, and listen around hootches where suspected VC lived. Once in a while we got lucky and bagged a few. In 2-1-5, we had a refugee village in our AO that had quite a few VC sympathizers, and we shot a few trying to get out at night and signal the enemy.

Then one day we received orders not to call them killer teams anymore; they were now known as security teams. *Killer team* was too harsh a term, I guess. Sure made me feel a lot better.

Every so often an officer from the rear would join us for a night ambush when our CAP was making a lot of contact. All he wanted to do was earn his CAR [Combat Action Ribbon], and then we never saw him again. What a bunch of phonies.

I was in one compound that was almost overrun, and the only reason I was there was I had a fever and they kept me out of the bush for one night. I thought, Oh boy, a night to relax.

About one o'clock in the morning the shit hits the fan. The enemy is in the wire. They assigned me to the second line of defense, which was a machine gun on a commo bunker with some guy I didn't know. It was a mixed bag manning the perimeter: Marines and Army personnel, plus the PFs. They pulled back but we repulsed the assault. In the morning there were over 100 dead NVA bodies scattered everywhere. We suffered about 60 or so dead and wounded, mostly ARVN, PFs, and a few Army MACV personnel. Some night of rest!

Warren Carmon holds a B40 rocket, found days after an attack on his compound.

Most of our PFs were not dependable at all, but we did have one Kit Carson scout—we called him Hawkeye because the top part of his eyelid was missing—who seemed to know what was going to happen before it did. I hate to think what happened to him after the war. Of course, I hate to think what happened to most of 'em after we left. Boy . . . we left 'em hangin'. Peace with honor? I don't think most of us bought that. I know I didn't. What a joke.

We moved around so much I can never remember the names of most of the villages. Maybe I don't want to remember. The people, at least to your face, were very friendly. They encouraged us to stay around their homes to protect them. We got along great with the kids. I used to pay one of them to run errands for me, wash my clothes, things like that. I had my mother send a pair of Levis for him. I think he was the best-dressed kid in all of Vietnam.

I was wounded not by the enemy, but by friendly fire. We were mortared one morning courtesy of the U.S. Army. We could actually hear them being launched from their tubes and knew they were ours. When you're in the bush for a while you can hear the difference in the sound. We really didn't disperse, which was a big mistake. Before we knew it eighteen rounds hit all around us. I took some shrapnel in the leg—nothing serious, but it hurt like hell.

But the Army wasn't the only service that made mistakes with friendly fire: the Marines did it too. One time this Marine firebase accidentally hit a MACV and a CAP compound, killing several PFs and a black Army sergeant. This black sergeant always tried to help our CAP whenever possible, and then he gets killed by Marine fire. We felt real bad. I hope the Army spared his family the truth about the incident. I think it's better to let them think the enemy did it.

We fought hard, and we fought for each other. No ideals, although I believe CAP Marines were a lot more idealistic than the others who served in Vietnam. CAPs were tight, for the most part. I remember guys not wanting to go on R and R because it would leave the platoon shorthanded. We felt a responsibility to the people and our fellow Marines.

It's funny, you counted the days until you rotated back to the States, but when it came your time to go, you really didn't want to. You belonged. That was a common feeling among CAP Marines. It was very confusing.

Was the CAP program successful? Well, the whole Vietnam experience wasn't very successful. But the CAPs were, in part at least. A lot of good people died for nothing, though.

★　　★　　★

Warren Carmon is single and lives in Pittsfield, Massachusetts. He is employed by an oil company and travels a great deal. He would like to move to Alaska someday.

L. Cpl. Paul Hernandez, USMC (Ret.)

2d CAG
1970–1971

A resident of Brady, Texas, Paul Hernandez enlisted in the Marine Corps immediately following high school in 1969. He was assigned to CAPs 2-7-2 and 2-7-10 near Hoi An.

We flew into Da Nang on an American Airlines flight and they put us in transit barracks for a couple of days. Another Marine and I, Channing Richard Protho from Aubrey, Texas, were selected to go to a CAG unit. We didn't even know what a CAG was or meant. They transported us to CAG headquarters and gave us temporary quarters. All the "old salts" rotating back to the States stopped in and told us some real horror stories about the CAPs. They kept telling us how they were being overrun. These war stories began to get to us and we contemplated asking for a transfer, but we decided to stick it out and see what these CAPs were all about.

Once we completed CAP school we were sent to Hoi An, the 2d CAG headquarters. We stood tower watches for about a week while awaiting orders to our respective platoons. We were sitting on the front steps of our barracks one day when we heard a shot go off. We ran inside to discover that a black CAP Marine had committed suicide. He had placed his rifle underneath his chin and pulled the trigger. It was awful. His brains were scattered all over the place. That was the first time we had confronted death since arriving in country, and it scared us. Apparently this individual had completed his tour and was going home. He left a note to his father that said in effect that he could never measure up to him and would be ridiculed about his service in Vietnam. He couldn't handle that. This shocked us. We realized this was a place of death and we weren't the little kids we had been just a few months before. We would soon lose our values and become immune to the death and killing. All that mattered was survival.

I was assigned to CAP 2-7-10, which received quite a bit of enemy traffic. On our day patrols we encountered a lot of booby traps. There was this one railroad tie we crossed over every day on patrol. On our return trip, instead of changing our pattern, we came back the same way. One day the tie blew; it was detonated from inside the ville. Three Marines were wounded and one lost his hearing. I would have been the next one to cross over it.

Every day we were under sniper fire while on patrols. One day we killed two VC, caught them going in a tunnel by the river. Another guerrilla we shot was still alive but seriously wounded. He just stared blankly at us. He never cried out in pain, just looked at us without uttering a sound. He seemed to be saying, "You can't hurt me, I'm dead already. And there's a lot more to follow me." They were tough little bastards, I can attest to that.

Part of what keeps that one day so clear in my mind is the way we took the two dead VC out of there. We tied their hands and feet together and put a pole between them and carried them out to Highway 1. It was like we had killed an animal. We dumped them right on the main road as a reminder to people of what happens to VC sympathizers. I guess we had become hardened by the war and we were proud of our catch. It was like going hunting, except we were after human prey.

The field was our home. We picked a day haven where we ran our patrols, sometimes two or three a day. Our main mission was to prevent the VC from stealing the farmers' rice and harassing them. One way of knowing if the VC were in the area was to keep an eye on the vats the farmers kept their rice in. If they were empty, Charlie had passed through. The farmers would never tell us anything, so we didn't know if we were helping them or hindering them. It was very frustrating.

In the evening we set up in night defensive positions, usually near the ville. We had quite a few snipers after darkness. Our CAP selected two or three alternate sites and we kept moving, sometimes three or four times a night. We always told our CP, just in case we needed air or arty. We were all cross-trained in the weapons we had: the M-60 machine gun, the M-79, and we were all familiar with radio procedure. These things were imperative for survival in a firefight.

One night we established our site in a graveyard. A Marine went to move between one of the mounds [the Vietnamese bury their dead sitting up] and a bush, and he set off a grenade that was

L. Cpl. Paul
Hernandez

171

L. Cpl. Paul Hernandez, locked and loaded

in a can and tied to a string. When he tripped it he turned toward the blast and received a serious chest wound. We tried desperately to place cigarette wrappers on the gaping hole in his chest. I was holding him. We got a medevac immediately. He was still alive when we put him on the chopper, but he died several days later. It took me a while to stop thinking about how he died.

Then we got a new squad leader. Another Marine, Prentiss Waltman from Florida, and I didn't think he knew what he was doing, and we requested a transfer. Two Marines had gotten killed in CAP 2-7-2 so Captain Mallard, our CACO commander, put us there. He was a hard man but fair, and we all respected him for that.

I was involved in more firefights in my new CAP, probably because it was nearer to the river and used as a VC infiltration route. I ran into my brother-in-law there, Doc Sanchez, a Navy corpsman from Sonora, Texas. We tried to get put in the same unit but we were denied. He was in CAP 2-7-4, right across the road, and we got to see each other all the time anyway. It was good to be near someone from home.

We all became real tight. Everybody had a nickname; I was Tex. Because there were only ten or twelve of us, there was a tremendous camaraderie. Even our Navy corpsman was thought of as a Marine. We all depended on each other for our lives.

Once we uncovered a tunnel system the VC used. They'd pop out of their spider holes, let off a few rounds, and burrow back in the tunnel, which took them to the river. We never saw who was shooting at us, but we eventually blew all the holes. They even brought dogs out, but we never found any VC in the holes. While we were detonating these spider holes, I caught a few pieces of shrapnel in my legs. I was careless, I guess. The corpsman told me I rated a Purple Heart, but I thought it was embarrassing. I stayed in the field after he dressed my wounds. It was no big deal.

We were allowed in-country R and R at Hoi An every so many weeks because we spent so much time in the field. But nobody wanted to go there, because they made us do dirty jobs like burning the shitters [pouring kerosene on the half-cut fifty-five-gallon drums that were used as toilets and then putting a match to them], and they hassled us about shaving, putting on clean utilities, whatever they could find. And this was supposed to be R and R! I preferred to stay in the field where nobody bothered me.

Children were constantly around us. I loved the kids. They were real intelligent. It amazed me the way they lived. They seemed indifferent to the violence around them; death was a common occurrence. They were born into it. I had one little boy, Dum-Dum, who stayed with me quite a bit during the day. He'd run my errands, pull buckets out of the well so I could bathe, just a gofer. He was curious about the United States and asked a lot of questions in the little English he understood, but we managed to communicate. I still have his picture on my wall in the living room.

The weather was a big factor against us; it was always raining. Everything we did was in the rain. One of our favorite songs was by Creedence Clearwater Revival: "Who'll Stop the Rain?" We stayed wet. Ponchos and poncho liners were a valuable asset. And it was difficult to maintain personal hygiene. We set up numerous patrol sites in rice paddies and that's where the people went to the bathroom. When we received sniper rounds we'd have to hit the deck. That was really getting in the shit!

In our CAP we tried to avoid firefights and placing ourselves in dangerous situations where we could be overrun. Twelve Marines were certainly no match for any large VC or NVA unit. We did have PFs, ten or twelve sometimes. They never followed any of the rules. They'd light up a cigarette, sleep on watch, talk. We figured they were making noise to let the VC know we were coming. Our Kit Carson scout was good, though. We liked him; he knew what he was doing. He'd been trained by the North Vietnamese.

One of our daytime tasks was checking the ID cards of Vietnamese farmers. They were usually in plastic to keep them from becoming destroyed by the weather. The farmers would take clothespins and place them in a conspicuous spot on their clothing. We became familiar with most of the people so we'd recognize any stranger immediately. Any of the so-called farmers we'd catch without IDs were sent back to the rear. Our Kit Carson scout showed no mercy when he was interrogating a suspect.

At night we had a VC we nicknamed the Phantom Blooper. He seemed to work all the CAPs in our area, firing a few M-79 rounds at us and then disappearing. I'm sure he lived in our AO, but he traveled throughout the area. I don't think he was ever caught.

We were always ready to move to another CAP's AO if they needed us—we monitored the radio nets. This was known as a react [reactionary force]. We had to move at a moment's notice to help our sister CAPs, and anything could happen after dark.

If we saw any movement, it was fair game. The villagers had a curfew, so they knew the consequences of stepping out after sunset. We'd fire on any lights, also. We knew the VC used these as signals to move at night and infiltrate our area, and we knew some of the villagers were aiding the VC. For example, back in CAP 2-7-10 there was this one woman who sold us Cokes and then sat with us at our day haven until dark. Then she left. It took a while to dawn on us that every time she was around we got hit. She was picking up information from us without our realizing it. So we set her up: we purposely let her know where we were going to be that night, and we got ambushed. We did this several times, and every time we were hit. Well, needless to say, she was done away with. Not a very pretty sight, I can assure you.

Every so often several of us were allowed to go to Hoi An to see a USO show. It was nice, but also frustrating. All we ever looked at all day was Vietnamese women, and to see these round-eyed beauties prancing around in their bikinis was more than I could stand. Later one of the Vietnamese pimps would bring out his girls, but standing in line with fifteen other guys to wait for one girl just wasn't my idea of a good time. I was proud I never did it.

January 18, 1971, was the last day I ever walked. It was a normal day, and then we set up our night position near the village of Thanh Quit; I was on the radio. One of the PFs fell asleep, and instead of being the ambushers we were the ambushees. The VC shot me three times in the back while I was laying on my stomach, and I was immediately paralyzed. My legs felt like balloons. I vomited. Everything gets sketchy after that. I was medevaced to 1st Med Battalion in Da Nang, where one of the corpsman said, "You're filthy, Marine!" I thought, Well what did you expect?

My mother received some telegrams. The first was dated January 21, and it read: "Your son, LCpl Paul Hernandez, was wounded in Quang Nam Province, RVN. He sustained gunshot wounds to the chest and abdomen from hostile small arms fire." What's so odd about this is I was hit three times in the back, not the chest and abdomen.

I was air-evacuated to the United States on February 19 and admitted to U.S. Army Brook General Hospital in San Antonio, Texas. I didn't even know what paraplegia was, and I was paralyzed from the waist down.

Our company was the last to be deactivated, shortly after I was medevaced. I was proud to be in CAG. We were few, we were proud, and by God, we were Marines!

I was awarded the Navy Commendation Medal with Combat V for my service with the CAPs, especially for that patrol where I was wounded. The official report for that night showed that CAP 2-7-2 fired on ten VC. Two Marines, one Navy corpsman, and one Kit Carson scout were wounded. Four VC were killed, and three K54 pistols, one AK-47 rifle, seven M-26 grenades, and six Chicom [Chinese communist] grenades were captured.

When Tom Harvey, editor of the CAP Association newsletter, went back to Vietnam in 1989, he visited my old village of Thanh Quit. Tom was in the same ville two and a half years earlier, and we knew some of the same villagers. I asked him to look up Dum-Dum for me, and he found him. He was married with three kids but was only allowed to earn five dollars a month as a farmer.

Dum-Dum said he remembered me. After twenty-plus years it's a load off my mind to know he survived. He was a very special child, and I hate to think of all the hardships his family has had to endure. He couldn't pronounce Tex, so he used to say Tet. I can still hear him calling me.

★   ★   ★

L. Cpl. Paul Hernandez, USMC (Ret.), is active in civic affairs in his hometown of Brady, Texas. He was appointed to the Texas State Council by Governor Ann Richards and is a member of the School Board for the Brady Independent School District.

Wind-down
1969–1971

Conclusion

Sadly, the Combined Action Program never attained its long-term goal of pacification. The Viet Cong infrastructure was never completely destroyed, although aggressive CAP patrolling certainly disrupted the enemy's activities, and the PFs were never able to defend their villages alone. The corrupt South Vietnamese government totally alienated the people, enabling the VC to rally the peasant population to their side.

The CAPs had two major weaknesses, the first being the language barrier. Part of the problem may have been, as CAP Marine Michael Peterson says, that "there was no real attempt to systematically utilize enlisted graduates from the Defense Language School in Monterey, California" (1989, 24). Another CAP Marine, Warren Smith, waited a year before getting orders to Vietnam after having completed a ten-month language course.

The CAP's other major weakness was the selection process. All CAP Marines were supposed to be volunteers with six months of in-country combat experience, but such was not always the case, as the preceding chapters have illustrated.

In addition, and in all fairness to Westmoreland, the Marine Corps placed its own constraints on the program. There were approximately 80,000 Marines in Vietnam at the height of the war, but the Combined Action Program never exceeded 2,500 at any time. Only 4 percent of the total USMC force was allocated to the CAPs. It took two years for the CAPs to get a TO/E of their own!

And when the Marine Corps was winding down in Vietnam, why were the CAPs not expanded? Certainly pacification of the countryside was still a key concern. Why couldn't some of those qualified Marines in the 3d Marine Division who were interested in being reassigned to a CAP unit be allowed to transfer?

But realistically, it was probably too late. The time to push the program would have been in 1965, when the Marines first landed in force. By 1969 support for the war had waned and the American people wanted out of Vietnam.

Denying the enemy access to the rice-rich coastal areas where the majority of the population resides, forcing him to do battle on our terms, was the right strategy for victory in Vietnam. The Combined Action Program was a sound concept, but it took time. Pacification cannot be achieved overnight; it takes years.

Former CAP Marines disagree as to whether or not a Combined Action Program could be applied today in a Third World country. Michael Peterson's opinion is that "the CAPs originated in the Vietnam War and were unique to that war. The situation and the conditions may have been too unique to generalize the CAP concept into strategic doctrine" (Peterson 1989, 125–26).

But others, as we have seen, believe that it would work. However, appropriate people would have to be selected and trained, which is the key to any program of this nature. In Vietnam, the awesome responsibility entrusted to the CAP Marines can never be overstated. These teenagers, in most cases, were tasked with winning the confidence of a foreign people who distrusted and frequently hated them. This was a lot to ask of a Marine who had just left a line company and whose relationship with the Vietnamese was tenuous at best.

Sometimes, though, the idealistic attitude of an eighteen- or nineteen-year-old may have been an asset. Sometimes one person made the difference in determining whether the Vietnamese in a particular village would aid the CAP Marines assigned there.

The Combined Action Program was certainly the most imaginative strategy to emerge from the Vietnam conflict. And CAP-type units could indeed be used in low-intensity conflicts today, if the proper conditions were met.

Glossary

AID Agency for International Development

AK-47 Soviet-manufactured 7.62-mm assault rifle

AO Area of operations

APC Armored personnel carrier

Arty Slang for artillery

ARVN Army, Republic of Vietnam

B-40 Soviet-manufactured rocket-propelled grenade

Bac-Si Vietnamese word for *doctor*

BAR Browning automatic rifle

Blooper Slang for M-79 grenade launcher

C-4 Plastic explosive

C-rations Canned meals for use by combat troops in the field

CO Commanding officer

CP Command post

CAC or CACO Combined Action Company

CAF Combined Action Force

CAG Combined Action Group

CAP Combined Action Platoon, Combined Action Program

CAR Combat Action Ribbon

CUPP Combined Unit Pacification Program

CH-53 Sikorsky heavy cargo helicopter, also known as Sea Stallion

Charlie Slang term for the enemy used by U.S. troops

Chicom Chinese communist

Chieu Hoi Vietnamese phrase meaning *open arms*. A U.S. program that
encouraged enemy troops to defect and become scouts and interpreters
for allied forces

Civic action Military and civilian efforts to administer aid to the rural
population of South Vietnam

CORDS Civil Operations and Revolutionary Development Support

DMZ The demilitarized zone, where North and South Vietnam were
partitioned at the 17th parallel

Di-di Slang term for running away in combat

I Corps Pronounced "eye" Corps, the northernmost sector of South
Vietnam

FDC Fire direction center

FLC Force Logistics Command

Flak jacket Armored vest worn by U.S. forces to stop shrapnel

Flechettes Steel darts used in beehive rounds

FO Forward observer

Frag Fragmentation grenade

Free Fire Zone Area where a soldier can fire his weapon at a target without seeking permission

Grunt Slang term for infantryman

Huey Bell UH-1E attack and transport helicopter

Hootch Slang term for a Vietnamese farmer's dwelling

ITR Infantry Training Regiment

Illum Illumination grenade

KIA Killed in action

K-bar USMC fighting knife

Kit Carson Scout An NVA or VC who had defected and served as a scout and interpreter for U.S. forces

LP Listening post

LZ Landing zone

LAW M72, 66-mm light antitank weapon used against bunkers and other enemy fortifications

M-14 U.S.-manufactured 7.62-mm rifle

M-16 U.S.-manufactured 5.56-mm assault rifle

M-26 U.S.-manufactured hand grenade

M-60 U.S.-manufactured 7.62-mm light general-purpose machine gun that fired 600 rounds per minute

M-79 U.S.-manufactured 40-mm single-shot grenade launcher

MACV U.S. Military Assistance Command Vietnam

MAF Marine Amphibious Force

MAG Marine Air Group

MEDCAP Medical Civic Action Program

MOS Military occupational specialty

Merck Manual Medical handbook

Medevac Medical evacuation, usually performed by helicopter

NCO Noncommissioned officer

NCOIC Noncommissioned officer in charge

NVA North Vietnamese Army

OP Observation post

PF South Vietnamese Popular Force soldier

PRC-10 FM radio with a range of five to eight kilometers

PRC-25 FM radio that replaced the AN/PRC-10 with a range of twenty-five miles

Pos Position

Project 100,000 Department of Defense directive that required the different branches of the U.S. military to accept personnel in Category IV (low intelligence, convicted felons, drug users). Under normal conditions, these individuals would have been excluded from military service.

Puff the Magic Dragon U.S. Air Force World War II–era twin-engine C-47 Gooneybird aircraft, renamed AC-47 and equipped with three rapid-fire 7.62-mm Gatling guns that could expend 6,000 rounds per minute

RD Revolutionary development

RF Regional Forces

RPG Rocket-propelled grenade

RVN *or* RSVN Republic of South Vietnam

R and R Rest and recuperation

Seabees U.S. Navy Construction Battalion

782 gear USMC-issue combat gear

Short-timer Individual with little time remaining on his tour

Sky Slang term meaning to run

Song Vietnamese word for *river*

Spider hole NVA or VC fighting hole

Starlight scope Night vision image intensifier with a range of 300 to 400 meters

TAD Temporary attached duty

TAOR Tactical area of responsibility

TDY Temporary duty

TO/E Table of organization and equipment

Tet Largest annual Vietnamese holiday

Top First sergeant, master sergeant, or master gunnery sergeant

Tracer Round of ammunition that has been treated so it glows in the dark and its path can be seen

Trung-si Vietnamese word meaning *sergeant*

UH-34D Sikorsky Sea Horse medium-cargo helicopter

VC Viet Cong

Vietnamization Term coined by Secretary of Defense Melvin Laird in 1969. It was a program that gradually turned the war over to the South Vietnamese while U.S. troops were withdrawing from South Vietnam.

Viet Minh Communist troops that fought the French and Japanese, later called Viet Cong

WIA Wounded in action

WesPac Western Pacific

Willie Peter white phosphorous

Bibliography

Corson, William R., Lt. Col., USMC (Ret.). *The Betrayal*. New York: 183 W. W. Norton & Co., 1968.

Cosmas, Graham A., and Lt. Col. Terrence P. Murray, USMC. *U.S. Marines in Vietnam: Vietnamization and Redeployment, 1970–1971*. Washington: History and Museums Division, Headquarters USMC, 1986.

Hammel, Eric. *Fire in the Streets: The Battle for Hue, Tet 1968*. Chicago: Contemporary Books, 1991.

Krulak, Victor H., Lt. Gen., USMC (Ret.). *First To Fight: An Inside View of the U.S. Marine Corps*. Annapolis: Naval Institute Press, 1984.

Lewandoski, Andrew S. *An Evaluation of the Combined Action Program in Vietnam*. New Haven: Yale University, May 14, 1991. Unpublished thesis.

Lewy, Guenter. *America in Vietnam*. New York: Oxford University Press, 1978.

McGonigal, Richard, Comdr., USN (Ret.). *Interim Report on Combined Action Units III MAF with Special Attention to Personal Relationships. Personal Response Project, FMF PAC (FWD)*. February 8, 1967.

Palm, Edward F., Maj., USMC. *Tiger Papa Three: A Memoir of the Combined Action Program, Parts I and II*. Quantico: *Marine Corps Gazette*, January 1988, 34–43; February 1988, 66–76.

Peterson, Michael E. *The Combined Action Platoons: The U.S. Marines' Other War in Vietnam*. New York: Praeger, 1989.

Shulimson, Jack. *U.S. Marines in Vietnam: An Expanding War, 1966*. Washington: History and Museums Division, Headquarters USMC, 1982.

Shulimson, Jack, and Maj. Charles M. Johnson, USMC. *U.S. Marines in Vietnam: The Landing and the Buildup, 1965*. Washington: History and Museums Division, Headquarters USMC, 1978.

Smith, Charles R. *U.S. Marines in Vietnam: High Mobility and Standdown, 1969*. Washington: History and Museums Division, Headquarters USMC, 1988.

Telfer, Gary L., Maj., USMC; Lt. Col. Lane Rogers, USMC; and Keith V. Fleming, Jr. *U.S. Marines in Vietnam: Fighting the North Vietnamese,*

1967. Washington: History and Museums Division, Headquarters USMC, 1984.

The Marines in Vietnam, 1954–1973: An Anthology and Annotated Bibliography. Washington: History and Museums Division, Headquarters USMC, 1974.

West, Francis J. *The Village*. New York: Harper & Row, 1972.

Westmoreland, William C., Gen., USA (Ret.). *A Soldier Reports*. Garden City, N.Y.: Doubleday, 1976.

Bibliography

Index

Index

189

About the Author

Born and raised in New Haven, Connecticut, Al Hemingway served with the Marines in Vietnam in 1969. He is the author of *Ira Hayes: Pima Marine* and is a senior editor for *Vietnam* magazine. He has three children, Brian, Michael, and Christopher, and resides in Waterbury, Connecticut.